# Spellbound
# Festive Beading

A Spellbound Bead Co Book
Copyright © Spellbound Bead Co Publishing 2010

First Published in the UK 2010
Reprinted 2011, 2012 & 2014

Julie Ashford has asserted her right to be identified as author
of this work in accordance with the Copyright, Designs and
Patents Act, 1988.

Printed in the UK by WM Print
for the Spellbound Bead Co


ISBN - 978-0-9565030-2-2

10  9  8  7  6  5  4


Editor:  Jean Hall
Pattern Testing and Sample Production:  Edna Kedge,
                    Pat Ashford & Erika Schrinner

Photography: Spellbound Bead Co


Visit our website at www.spellboundbead.co.uk

Spellbound Bead Co
47 Tamworth Street
Lichfield
Staffordshire
WS13 6JW
England


Call 01543 417650 for direct sales
or your local wholesale distributor

### Acknowledgements

A special thank you to everyone who has contributed to this book - those who have
tested, proofed and made cups of tea, taken photographs and counted beads.

Also a big thank you to all of our customers who have bought, made and given us
great feedback on all things bauble.  We hope that you enjoy the book.

A very special
thank you to Edna
Kedge who is the
very best bauble
beader and super-
efficient kit-tester
in the world.

# Contents

# Festive Beading

W e all love to decorate our homes in the festive season and a love for beading means
that the possibilities are endless.

I designed our first beaded bauble design, Swags &
Tails, over ten years ago, and it was received more
enthusiastically than I could possibly have hoped for.

Since then I have designed a new beaded bauble kit
every year alongside other kits for home decoration.
Tassels and stars made from beads of all shapes and
sizes have endless possibilities. I have made plain
beaded tassels, tumbling waterfalls and asymmetric
tassel designs, stars based on beading and stars based
on wirework, in 2D, in 3D and from small and delicate
to large statement pieces. From these and our ever
expanding range of beaded earrings I have chosen the
most popular festive designs that have been created
over the years and added two new bauble designs.
There are also several design ideas that are exclusive
to this book.

B ringing the designs together in this format has
also given me the chance to share with you
some of my ideas for taking the projects further
by adapting the designs. Just by changing the colours
you can get a completely different effect. You can
adapt the patterns for different sizes of bauble or turn
an element of a bauble fringe into the start of a new
jewellery design.

The Inspiration pages throughout the book point you in
new directions for the techniques learnt whilst making
the bauble designs. Some of these ideas are explored
in a little more detail, but in a shorter format than the
main projects. Read the Inspiration pages in conjunc-
tion with the main chapters and make sure you have
plenty of beads on hand to experiment, as with a little
lateral thinking, you can use the finished decorations
for mobiles, tags for presents or tassels for cabinet keys.

# Choose a Project to Suit Your Beading Experience

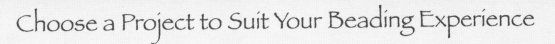

One Star - very easy - this project will be quick to make.

Two Stars - simple techniques - this project will take a little more time to complete.

Three Stars - getting a little more complex but manageable for a beginner with patience.

Four Stars - several stages building on top of one another. Each stage is straightforward, but there are more of them to follow, so it takes longer to get the desired result.

The majority of the projects in this book use very basic equipment - just a needle and some beading thread. There are a couple of exceptions which are based on simple wirework so a pair of pliers will be needed just to finish off the connections.

All of the projects in the book are written in the same way that I approach workshop and kit instructions – from first principles. All of the main projects have full step-by-step instructions and there are lots of photos to give you ideas for new colourways.

The designs are graded for difficulty (see above) to help you to choose between a 'quick and easy' and a 'longer sit down' project. If you have not done any beadwork before try one of the more simple projects first as they will make up quite quickly.

Throughout the book I have tried to use only readily available beading materials – there being nothing so frustrating as finding the perfect project and then being unable to find the beads to make it with!

Look out for the Extra Info boxes. They contain hints and tips on the techniques and materials you will be using in the projects.

I have had a fantastic time putting together this collection, as have the people who have helped to bring it all together via baubling, beading and red-penning their way through every corner of the manuscript before it was allowed to go to the printers. I hope you enjoy making the projects as much as I have designing them and you get many hours of joy from the finished pieces.

*Julie*

August 2010

# Essential Ingredients

The projects in this book all use a very simple selection of beads. For most of the designs you will need two sizes of seed beads, one size of bugle beads and a selection of fire polished faceted beads. This quick guide will give you an introduction to these basic supplies and the few extra items you might need for some of the patterns.

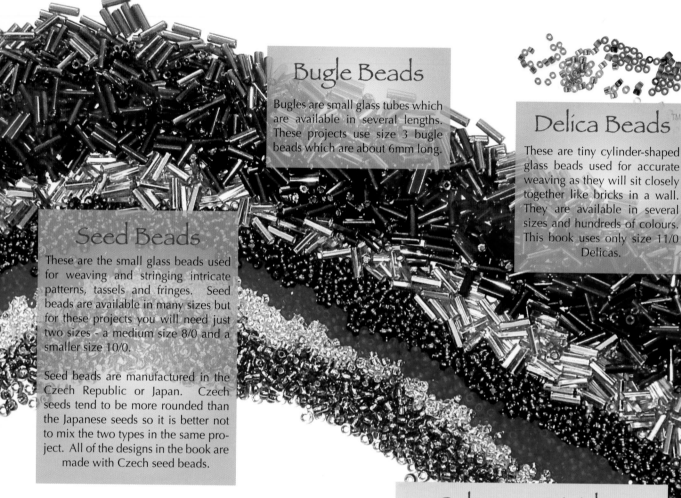

## Bugle Beads

Bugles are small glass tubes which are available in several lengths. These projects use size 3 bugle beads which are about 6mm long.

## Delica Beads™

These are tiny cylinder-shaped glass beads used for accurate weaving as they will sit closely together like bricks in a wall. They are available in several sizes and hundreds of colours. This book uses only size 11/0 Delicas.

## Seed Beads

These are the small glass beads used for weaving and stringing intricate patterns, tassels and fringes. Seed beads are available in many sizes but for these projects you will need just two sizes - a medium size 8/0 and a smaller size 10/0.

Seed beads are manufactured in the Czech Republic or Japan. Czech seeds tend to be more rounded than the Japanese seeds so it is better not to mix the two types in the same project. All of the designs in the book are made with Czech seed beads.

## Colours & Finishes

Crystal - a transparent plain glass that can have further effects added to it such as silver lined or AB.
Silver Lined - a metallic silver deposit on the inside of the hole which glistens through the glass and makes the beads sparkle more vibrantly.
AB - Aurora Borealis is a thin rainbow effect applied on top of the glass bead for extra glitz.
Frost - an acid-etched matt finish applied to a glass bead.
Ceylon - a pearlescent finish applied to a glass bead.

## Fire Polished Faceted Glass

To make a fire polished facet you must first make a round glass bead. Faceted faces are then ground away, one at a time, from the surface of the glass before the beads are placed in a kiln to 'fire polish'. The heat of the kiln is just hot enough to make the glass glaze over into a high shine.

More economical than cut crystal beads they are readily available in many sizes, colours and finishes.

Plastic Faceted Beads look similar to fire polished facets but are more lightweight and have a slightly larger hole.

## Cut Crystal Beads

Precision cut from very high quality lead crystal glass these faceted beads give a maximum amount of sparkle. You can substitute these beads with fire polished facets.

## Findings

You will need just a few items to complete the projects in the earring chapter:

Fishhook Earwires are comfortable to wear but you can substitute post & ball or clip earfittings if you prefer.

Jump Rings are the connecting links used in all sorts of jewellery designs.

## Sieves

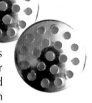

These perforated metal or plastic discs are usually used for bringing together clusters of beads into brooch or stud earring designs. They are available in many sizes and hole counts - if you cannot get the same count as specified in the project get the closest you can and adjust the bead recipe accordingly.

## Filigree Bead Cups

Usually used at either end of a bead to provide a filigree flourish to the design. We also use them at the top of tassels. Available in many diameters and metal finishes.

## Glass Donuts

Large washer-shaped beads usually used for pendants.

## Wire

Wire is commonly available but you need to make sure you pick the correct size and hardness as stated in the project.

Half-Hard Wire is used for structural shapes where it is important that the wire holds the shape firmly.

Soft Wire is used for weaving as it will snake through the bead patterns with ease.

## Beading Thread

Sold under many brand names such as Nymo and Superlon, beading thread is available in several thicknesses and many colours. These projects all use a size D thread.

# ~ Tools & Useful Extras ~

# Threading Necessities

## Beading Needles

Beading needles have a very slim eye so they can pass through a bead with a small hole.

Size 10 Beading is a general beading needle that is suitable for most of the projects.

Size 13 Beading is a little finer for multiple passes of the thread through the bead holes.

Sharp Scissors to trim the threads closely are essential.

A Thread Conditioner such as Thread Heaven helps to smooth the kinks in the thread if you get into a knot or tangle.

A Fleecy Bead Mat with a slight pile will stop the beads from rolling around and it makes it easy to pick up small beads with the point of the needle.

Clear Nail Polish is sometimes used to stiffen selected areas of stitched beadwork so that the desired shape is retained more firmly.

## Pliers

You will need pliers for the projects using wire and findings.

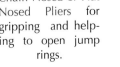

Round Nosed Pliers for turning loops.

Cutters for trimming wire to length.

Chain Nosed or Flat Nosed Pliers for gripping and helping to open jump rings.

# Tips & Techniques

There are a few basic techniques that you will need to work through the projects in the book. If you need a special technique for a particular project it will be explained within that chapter but for the techniques that apply to most of the designs this is what you need to read.

## Using a Keeper Bead

Before you start a piece of beadwork you will need to put a stopper at the end of the thread. The easiest stopper to use is a keeper bead. A keeper bead is a spare bead, ideally of a different colour to the work, that is held on a temporary knot close to the end of the thread. Once the beading is completed the keeper bead is removed. That end of the thread is then knotted securely and finished neatly within the beadwork pattern.

fig 1

To Add a Keeper Bead - Position the keeper bead 15cm from the end of the thread (unless instructed otherwise) and tie a simple overhand knot about the bead (fig 1). When you thread on the first beads of the pattern push them right up to the keeper bead - this tension in the thread will prevent the keeper bead from slipping. When the work is complete untie the knot and remove the keeper bead. Attach the needle to this end of the thread and secure as below.

## Finishing off a Thread End

You will need to finish off a thread end neatly and securely.

Pass the needle through a few beads of the pattern. At that position pick up the thread between the beads with the point of the needle. Pull the needle through to leave a loop of thread 2cm in diameter. Pass the needle through the loop twice (fig 2) and gently pull down to form a double knot between the beads.

fig 2

Pass the needle through five or six beads of the pattern and repeat the double knot. Pass the needle through five or six more beads before trimming the thread end as closely as possible to the work.

## Knotty Problems

Be careful where you tie your knots when adding a new thread into your work. Do not position the knots adjacent to, or inside beads, that you have to pass the needle through again because it will not fit through a hole blocked with thread.

## A Note About Baubles

Baubles are made by many different manufacturers - some are hand blown in paper-thin glass and others are machine-made in both glass and plastic.

Hand blown baubles can vary a little in size from the stated diameter so you may need to make a slight bead count adjustment if you are making a tightly fitted design. The variety of neck sizes across all diameters of baubles, both hand-made and machine-made, is quite marked. Most of the designs in the book require a closely fitted ring of beads around the neck so you may need to adjust your bead count accordingly. Guidance is given where necessary if you need to make adjustments.

## Starting a New Thread

On occasion you will need to add a new thread into the work.

Work the old thread until you have no less than 15cm of thread remaining. Remove the needle from this thread end and leave the end hanging loose. Prepare the needle with a new thread and tie a keeper bead 5cm from the end.

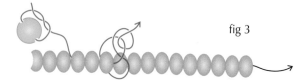

fig 3

Starting about 15 beads back from the old end of the thread pass the needle through 3 - 4 beads towards the old thread end. Make a double knot here (fig 3). Pass the needle through a further 4 - 5 beads and repeat the knot. Pass the needle through to emerge alongside the old thread end and continue the beading. When you have worked on a little you can trim away the keeper bead at the end of this thread. Return to the old thread end and reattach the needle. Finish off this end as in "Finishing off a Thread End'.

## Correcting a Mistake

If you make a mistake whilst you are following a pattern re-move the needle and pull the thread back until you have undone the work sufficiently. Do not turn the needle and try to pass it back through the holes in the beads - the needle tip will certainly catch another thread inside the beads and make a filamentous knot that is almost impossible to undo successfully.

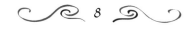

# Brick Stitch for Beginners

The Santa and Christmas Tree earring designs use brick stitch. If you have not used this technique before it is a good idea to make a sampler ten beads x ten rows just to familiarise yourself with how the stitch works. Try out an increase and a decrease as well so you are prepared to follow the pattern accurately.

Brick stitch is so called because of the pattern the beads form as they line up, in staggered rows, giving the impression of a brick wall. It can form flat pieces or cylinders but both require a starter row or 'foundation row' onto which the first row of brick stitch is worked.

**1** The Ladder Stitched Foundation Row - This ladder of beads is worked so that all the holes of the beads are lined up perpendicular to the length of the row.

Prepare the needle with 1.5m of single thread and tie a keeper bead 15cm from the end. Thread on two beads. Pass the needle back up through the first bead and down through the second to bring the two beads alongside one another (fig 1).

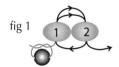

**2** Thread on a third bead; pass the neeedle back down bead 2 and back up bead 3 (fig 2) bringing bead 3 to sit alongside beads 1 and 2. Repeat for seven further beads to give you a row of ten (fig 3).

**3** Starting to Brick Stitch - Thread on two beads (11 & 12). Pick up the loop of thread between beads 10 and 9 and pass back up through bead 12 in the opposite direction (fig 4). This should bring the two new beads to sit alongside one another with bead 11 slightly overhanging the previous row.

**4** Thread on bead 13. Pick up the loop of thread between beads 9 and 8 and pass back up bead 13 (fig 5). Repeat adding one bead at a time to the end of the row (ten beads in total).

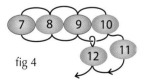
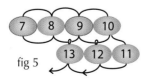

**5** Pick up beads 21 and 22 to start the next row (fig 6) and work to the end of the row. Continue to work a further seven rows. Each row starts with a two bead stitch followed by eight single bead stitches.

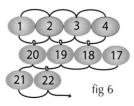

The beads of each row should sit right alongside one another and the rows should sit closely on top of one another. You should not be able to see the thread except at the top and bottom of the piece.

If you study the patterns for the Santa or Tree earrings you will see that the pattern steps in and out to shape the motif.

**6** Decreasing at the End of the Row - Finish the previous row as indicated on the pattern. The needle will now need to be repositioned for the first stitch of the new row. Study the pattern and decide which bead on the row just worked lies between the first two beads on the new row - this is the bead through which the needle must emerge to start the new row.

Pass the needle back along the row just worked, up and down, through the beads until you reach the correct starting bead. If you emerge on the leading edge of the work you can resume the beading with the first two beads of the new row (fig 7). However, if you emerge with the needle pointing towards the main body of the work you will need to turn the needle around through the beads of the previous row (fig 8).

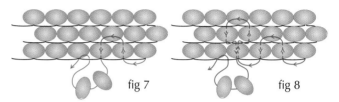

Start the new row with the first two beads of the pattern. Use this method of turning the needle through the beads of the previous row if you just need to start the row one bead in from the edge to avoid the overhanging bead at the beginning of a standard row (fig 9).

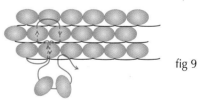

This method of repositioning the needle to start the beading in the correct position, with the needle pointing in the correct direction, to begin the stitch, is the main skill required to make a success of any brick stitch project.

**7** Increasing at the End of the Row - Pick up one bead and pass the needle back down through the last bead of the row. Pass back up through the increase bead (fig 10) - this is just like making the foundation row. You can continue to add beads to the end of the row with the same method if the pattern requires it (fig 11).

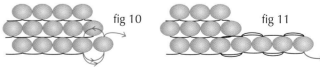

If necessary reposition the needle as for the decreasing technique before you start the new row.

If you do need to add extra beads to the start of a row you will need to work the beads that are attached to the previous row first; then backtrack up and down through the beads just added to the start of the row. Add the beads to the start of the row as above.

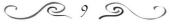

# Crystalline Snowflake

## You Will Need

### Materials

4g of size 8/0 silver lined crystal seed beads A
2g of size 3 silver lined bugle beads B
Thirteen 6mm faceted plastic beads C
Six 4mm faceted plastic beads D
2m of 0.2mm soft beading wire

### Tools

A pair of old scissors or
wire cutters to trim the wire

The snowflake design is the easiest and quickest make in the collection. Keep the wire smooth as you work and don't pull too hard - you just need the beads to come up snugly to one another - a bit of wire will show between the beads here and there. These make great card decorations; tags for special gifts and festive decorations for mobiles - see page 13 for more ideas.

**1** Cut 25cm of wire - put this short piece aside for now. Take the remaining 1.75m piece and rub right down the length with your fingers to remove any kinks.

**2** Approximately 30cm from the end of the long piece of wire thread on 2A, 1D, 2A, 1C and 1A. Thread one C onto the long end of the wire and pass the short end through the same bead in the opposite direction to form a loop of beads (fig 1). Pull the ends of the wire to bring the beads together snugly (fig 2).

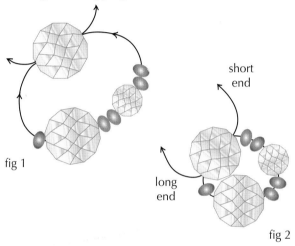

fig 1

short end

long end

fig 2

**3** Thread onto the shorter end of the wire 2A, 1D and 2A. Thread onto the long end 1A and 1C. Pass the short end of the wire the opposite way through the new C bead to make a second loop (fig 3).

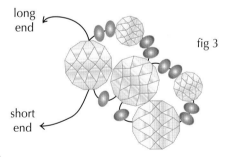

long end

fig 3

short end

**4** For the next loop thread the bead sequence that you have just put onto the short wire onto the long one and vice versa crossing the wires over in the C bead as before (fig 4).

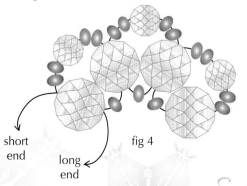

short end

long end

fig 4

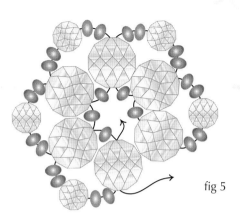

fig 5

**5** You now need to make a further two loops swapping the bead sequences to and fro to make five loops that bend around into an almost complete circle, with the D beads on the edge, and the single A beads to the centre (fig 5). To complete the circle thread 2A, 1D and 2A onto the short wire and 1A onto the longer wire - pass the two ends of the wire in opposite directions through the first C bead of the first loop (fig 6).

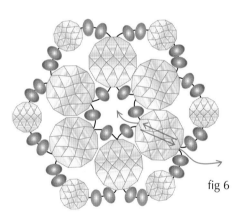

fig 6

**6** Reposition the long end of the wire by threading it up through the adjacent 2A and 1D beads (fig 7). Finish off the short end of the wire by wrapping around the wire between two adjacent beads and trimming neatly.

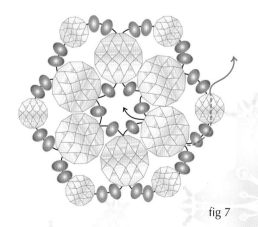

fig 7

A very similar pattern but with much smaller beads (3mm crystal bicones, size 15/0 seeds and Delicas) on thread to make tiny earrings.

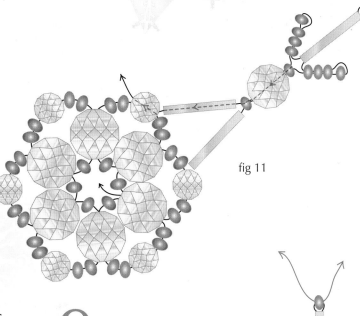

fig 11

**7** Thread on 1B, 1A, 1C and 5A. Push the beads right up to the D bead on the ring.

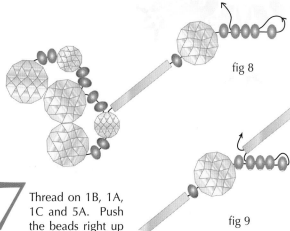

fig 8

fig 9

Leaving aside the last A bead threaded to act as a stopper; pass the wire back down the next 3A just threaded to make a bead spike (fig 8). Thread on 1B and 1A. Leaving aside the last 1A threaded pass the wire back down the B bead (fig 9) to make a second bead spike.

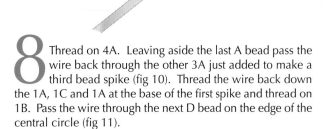

fig 10

**8** Thread on 4A. Leaving aside the last A bead pass the wire back through the other 3A just added to make a third bead spike (fig 10). Thread the wire back down the 1A, 1C and 1A at the base of the first spike and thread on 1B. Pass the wire through the next D bead on the edge of the central circle (fig 11).

Repeat figs 8 to 11 five times to complete the six arms of the snowflake. Finish off the tail of the wire as before.

### Extra Info.....
If you find it difficult to pass the wire end back through the beads try attaching the end of the wire to a needle - 0.2mm wire will just fit through the eye of a size 10 beading needle.

**9** Go back to the 25cm of wire put aside in step 1. Thread this through the central A bead at the end of one of the arms (fig 12) so the snowflake hangs from the centre of the 25cm piece of wire. Thread 3A onto each end of the wire. Bring the two ends of the wire together and thread on 1C.

Separate the wire ends and add 20A to each end of the wire.

Twist the two ends of the wire together to complete the loop. Pass the two wire ends in opposite directions through the beads to either side of the twist to neaten the join and trim closely.

fig 12

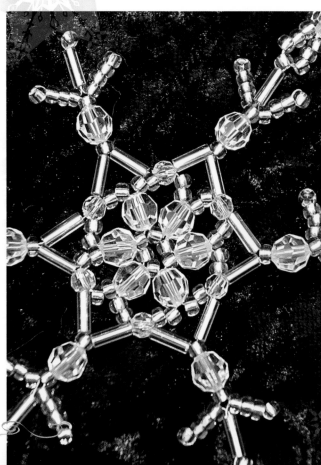

## Try Making a Mobile for the Window

Here we have added Sirius Stars and Aurora Stars to the Snowflakes for a sparkly extravaganza. The danglers are all suspended on clear nylon thread.

To make a mobile hanger you will need 25cm of 1.2mm half-hard wire.

Make a loop in the centre (fig 1).

fig 1

fig 2

fig 3

Curl each end around a 2cm diameter former (like a thick marker pen) (fig 2).

Use round nosed pliers to draw the centre of the curl into a loop (fig 3).

Here we have used the snowflake as a decorative tag on a special gift. They make a great motif on a greetings card too.

13

# Aurora Stars

## You Will Need

### Materials

Forty-two 4mm fire polished faceted beads A
3g of size 3 silver lined bugle beads B
Twelve 6mm fire polished faceted beads C
3g of size 8/0 silver lined seed beads D
60cm of 0.8mm half hard silver plated wire
50cm of clear nylon thread
A reel of white size D beading thread

### Tools

A size 10 beading needle
A pair of scissors to trim the threads
A pair of wire cutters
A pair of round nosed pliers

This three dimensional star is quick to make which is a great advantage as they look great when hung in profusion on the tree or from candlesticks on the mantlepiece. Stars are not just for Christmas though - think about making a mobile for the window, for decorations at a special party or use them to hold place setting cards on the dinner table.

The Decoration is Made in Two Stages
First an openwork sphere is stitched from the 4mm beads.
Lengths of wire then thread through the holes to make the points of the star.

**1** The Sphere - Prepare the needle with 1.2m of thread; bring the two ends together to double up the thread and tie a keeper bead 15cm from the cut ends.

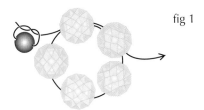

fig 1

**2** Thread on 5A. Pass the needle through the first 2A again to bring the five into a ring (fig 1). Thread on 4A. Pass the needle through the A bead on the first ring that the needle emerged from to bring the new beads into a ring alongside the first (fig 2). Pass the needle through the first A bead of the 4A just added (fig 3).

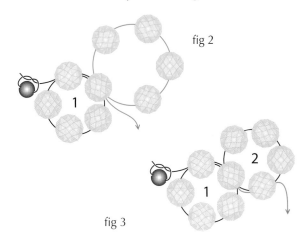

fig 2

fig 3

**3** Thread on 3A. Pass the needle through the third A of the first ring and the adjacent A bead of the second ring followed by the first A of the 3A just added (fig 4). This makes the third ring.

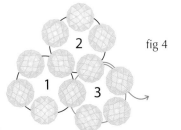

fig 4

**4** Thread on 3A. Pass the needle through the second A bead of the second ring and the first A bead of the third ring followed by the first of the 3A just added (fig 5). This makes the fourth ring.

Try to pull the threads as tightly as you can. You will see that the beadwork will not lie flat, and indeed, it curves quite a bit.

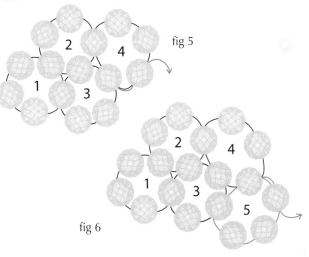

fig 5

fig 6

**5** Thread on 3A. Pass the needle through the second A bead of the third ring and the first A bead of the fourth ring followed by the first of the 3A just added (fig 6).

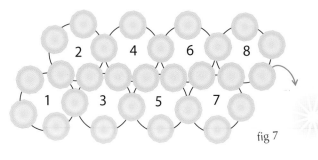

fig 7

**6** Repeat step five three more times to add a sixth ring to the fourth and fifth one; a seventh one to the fifth and sixth; and an eighth to the sixth and seventh ring to make eight rings in total (fig 7).

**7** The ninth ring joins the seventh and eighth ring to the first ring. As before make sure that you have finished the eighth ring by passing the needle through the first of the 3A just added. Thread on 1A. Pass the needle through the fifth A bead of the first ring (marked W on fig 8); thread on 1A; pass the needle through the second A bead of the seventh ring and the first A bead of the eighth. Pass the needle through the first A bead just added to complete the ring (fig 8).

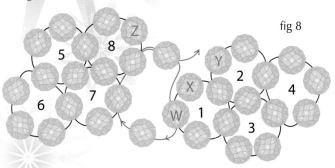

fig 8

**8** Pass the needle up through the A beads marked X and Y on fig 9 and thread on 1A. Pass the needle down through the A bead marked Z and the first A bead of the ninth ring to complete the tenth ring (fig 9).

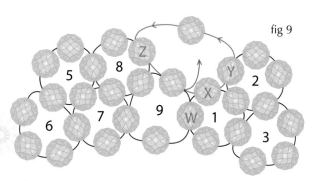

fig 9

**9** If you examine the sphere you will see that there are 5A beads forming an extra ring to either side of the strip of 10 rings just completed. Run the needle through these five beads at each side of the sphere to firm up the whole shape (fig 10). Finish off the thread end by picking up the threads between two adjacent beads; fastening off the needle thread to these threads and passing the needle through a few beads before trimming. Remove the keeper bead; reattach the needle to this end and finish off similarly.

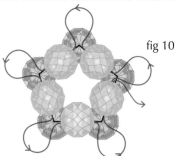

fig 10

**10** Adding The Points - Cut the 0.8mm wire into six 10cm pieces. Using your round nosed pliers make a 3mm diameter loop at one end of all six wires. Onto the first wire thread 1D, 1B, 1D, 1A, 1D and 1C. Pass the end of the wire into one of the rings of the sphere and out through the ring on the opposite side of the void in the centre. Thread on 1C, 1D, 1A, 1D, 1B and 1D.

## Making a Loop

A finished loop should be round, properly closed and centred on the end of the wire or pin. You will need to use a pair of round nosed pliers to make a good loop.

Round nosed pliers taper towards the tip - the closer to the tip you grip the wire the smaller the finished loop will be. Individual pairs of pliers will vary but for a loop 3mm in diameter you will need to use the pliers quite close to the tips (about 2mm from the end).

Grip the very end of the wire with your round nosed pliers. Hold the wire with your other hand 8mm down from the pliers (fig a) - the wire will bend between the pliers and your other hand so make sure the spacing is correct.

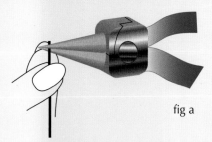

fig a

Keep the wire still and roll your plier wrist over. The wire will start to bend (fig b) - do not over-rotate your wrist. Grip the wire with the pliers at the apex of the bend and with your other hand back in the same place on the wire roll the pliers again until the loop closes up (figs c & d).

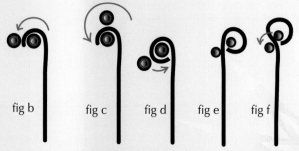

fig b     fig c     fig d     fig e     fig f

Using the very tips of the pliers grip the very bottom corner of the loop. With your other hand grip the wire immediately below the pliers. Roll the pliers back just a quarter of a turn to centralise the loop (figs e & f).

**11** Trim the excess wire length down to 8mm and, making sure that the C beads are nestling down into the rings in the sphere, turn a loop at the end of the wire to secure it (fig 11).

Repeat with the other five wires until you have assembled a twelve pointed 3-D star.

fig 11

Use the clear nylon thread to suspend the star.

# Sirius Stars

This three-dimensional star is made with thread and beads alone. As it is so lightweight it can dangle from the branches on the tree, swing from a mobile, or be strung at intervals along a clear nylon thread for a garland. You might think they are too pretty to put away after the festivities so why not convert them into earrings or a pendant that can be worn all the year around.

This Decoration is Made in Two Stages
The first stage is to construct a ladder-stitched ring of crystal beads. The points of the star are then added to the ring to complete the design.

**1** The Ring - Prepare the needle with 1.5m of single thread and tie a keeper bead 15cm from the end. Thread on 1A, 2B, 1A and 2B. Pass the needle through the first A bead a second time to bring the beads into a loop with the two A beads parallel to one another (fig 1). Pass the needle through the following 2B and 1A (fig 2).

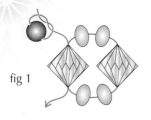

fig 1

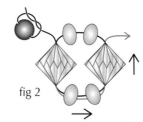

fig 2

**2** Thread on 2B, 1A and 2B. Pass the needle through the previous A bead to make a new loop (fig 3). Pass the needle through the following 2B and 1A of the new loop (fig 4).

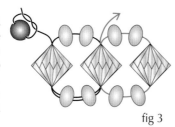

fig 3

Repeat step 2 two more times to give you five A beads in a row.

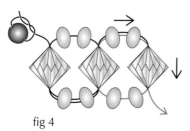

fig 4

**3** Thread on 2B. Referring to fig 5 pass the needle up through the first A bead of the sequence. Thread on 2B and pass down through the last A bead threaded to draw the work up into a ring (fig 5).

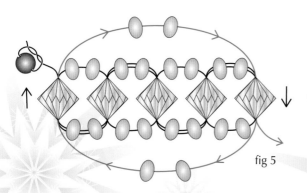

fig 5

**4** The ring needs to be reinforced. Pass the needle through the 10B beads at one end of the ring (fig 6). Repeat. Pass the needle through the closest A bead to reach the other end of the ring. Pass the needle through the B beads at this end of the ring twice.

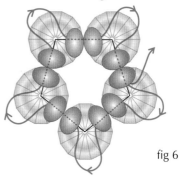

fig 6

Pass the needle through the closest A bead on the ring.

**5** The Points - Thread on 1C, 1B, 1A and 1B. Leaving aside the last B bead threaded to anchor the strand pass the needle back through the A bead and thread on 1B and 1C. Pass the needle through the A bead on the ring in the same direction as before (fig 7) to pull the new beads up into a triangular spike.

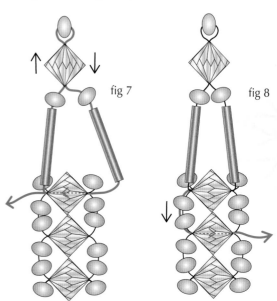

fig 7

fig 8

**6** Pass the needle through the next 2B beads around the ring and the following A bead (fig 8).

## Extra Info
The thread can build up quite quickly inside the beads when you are making a 3D shape and this can make it difficult to pass the needle through the holes. Always keep a few thinner needles on hand (size 13 are ideal) just in case - swapping the needle will save your hands and stop you from splitting the beads.

**7** Thread on 1C and 1B. Pass the needle up through the A bead at the top of the previous triangle and the following anchor bead (fig 9).

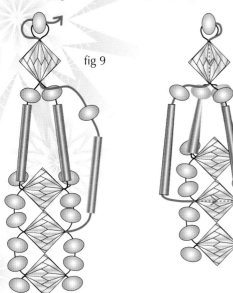

fig 9

fig 10

**9** The next point is constructed between the A bead that the needle is emerging from and the next A bead around the ring. Repeat steps 5 to 8 to make the next point of the star (fig 11).

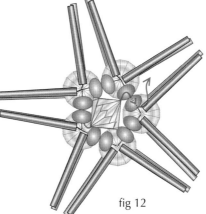

fig 11

Repeat three more times to complete the five points of the star.

**8** Pass the needle back through the A bead and thread on 1B and 1C. Pass the needle through the A bead at the base of the previous C bead in the same direction as before (fig 10) to make a new triangle that links to the previous triangle.

This completes the beading for this point of the star. If necessary adjust the tension in the thread so that the point sticks out firmly from the ring with the A bead at the top of the point standing vertical.

fig 12

**10** Pass the needle through one of the adjacent B beads and thread on 1A. Referring to fig 12 pass the needle through the B bead directly opposite the first B bead on the edge of the ring to pull the A bead across the centre of the space.

**11** Pass the needle through the adjacent A bead to the other side of the ring. Repeat step 10 to add the final A bead across the centre of the ring as fig 12. Finish off the thread end securely. Remove the keeper bead and secure this thread end in a similar fashion.

# Using The Sirius Star

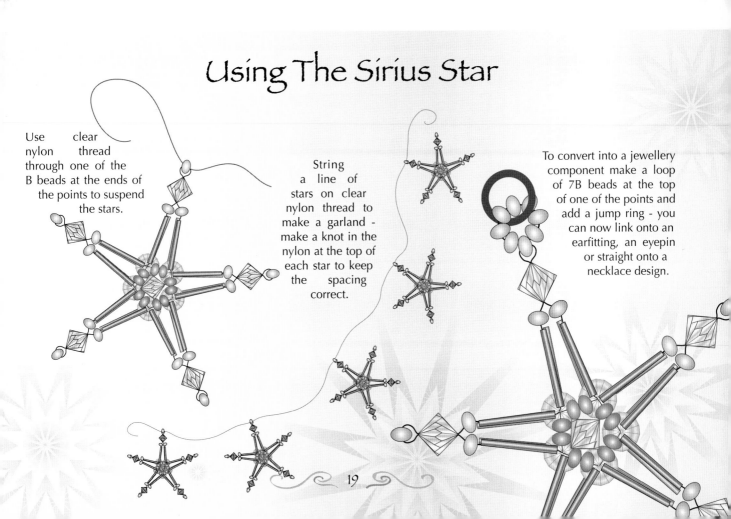

Use clear nylon thread through one of the B beads at the ends of the points to suspend the stars.

String a line of stars on clear nylon thread to make a garland - make a knot in the nylon at the top of each star to keep the spacing correct.

To convert into a jewellery component make a loop of 7B beads at the top of one of the points and add a jump ring - you can now link onto an earfitting, an eyepin or straight onto a necklace design.

# Art Deco Bauble

## You Will Need

### Materials

One 30mm frosted gold glass bauble
6g of size 10/0 silver lined gold seed beads A
3g of size 8/0 silver lined bronze seed beads B
Ten 6mm topaz rhomboidal glass beads C
Fourteen 4mm topaz fire polished faceted beads D
Two 8mm topaz fire polished faceted beads E
A reel of gold size D beading thread

### Tools

A size 10 beading needle
A pair of scissors to trim the threads

The Art Deco design fits closely over a 30mm bauble shape. As bead sizes vary very slightly and bauble diameters are not always precise you may need to make a little adjustment in the bead count to make the top section of the design fit properly. Guidance is given for this adjustment when necessary.

The Decoration is Made in Four Stages

The foundation row around the neck.
The tightly fitted net around the bauble.
The tassel strand from the base of the net.
The hanging loop at the top of the bauble.

**1** The Foundation Row - Prepare the needle with 2.5m of single thread and tie a keeper bead 15cm from the end. Thread on 3A and 1B seven times. Drape the beads around the neck of the bauble. If the beads do not meet together try with 2A or 4A between the B beads until you get a snug fit. When you have the best fit of A and B beads in seven repeats pass the needle through the ring of beads a second time to emerge after the first B bead of the ring (fig 1).

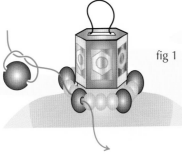

fig 1

**2** The Fitted Net - Thread on 6A, 1B, 4A, 1B, 4A, 1B and 6A. Pass the needle through the next B bead around the neck ring (fig 2). *Thread on 6A and pass the needle through the last B bead of the loop just made to bring the 6A beads parallel to the side of the last loop. Thread on 4A, 1B, 4A, 1B and 6A. Pass the needle through the next B bead around the foundation row (fig 3).
Repeat from * four more times to complete six interlinked loops dangling from the foundation row.

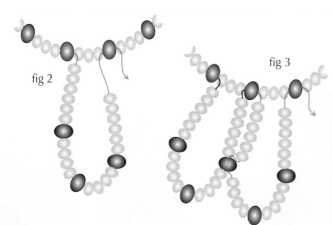

fig 2

fig 3

**3** For the last loop thread on 6A and pass the needle through the last B bead of the last loop as before. Thread on 4A, 1B and 4A. Pass the needle up through the first B bead of the first loop and thread on 6A. Pass the needle through the next B bead on the neck ring to complete the first row of netting. Pass the needle through the first 6A, 1B, 4A and 1B of the first loop to emerge through the B bead at the bottom of the loop. This is the correct position to start the next row.

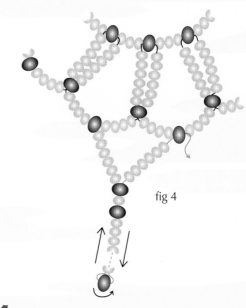

fig 4

**4** Thread on 6A, 1B, 1A, 1B, 8A and 1B. Turn the needle and leaving aside the last B bead threaded to anchor the strand pass the needle back up through the last 8A, 1B, 1A and 1B. Thread on 6A and pass the needle through the B bead at the bottom of the next loop around the foundation row (fig 4).
Repeat right around the bauble to complete seven loops each with a central dangling rod of beads.

**5** Pass the needle through the beads of the first loop on this row to emerge through the bottom B bead on the first rod. Pass the needle through the B bead at the base of the next rod around the bauble and the following five B beads at the bottom of the remaining five rods.

Pass the needle through the B bead at the bottom of the first rod again to bring the B beads into a ring (fig 5).

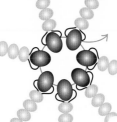

fig 5

Adjusting to Fit - The netting should now fit snugly over the bauble and the B beads at the bottom should come together in a tidy ring of 7B. If there is a large amount of thread showing between the B beads at the bottom of the bauble or the netting is very baggy over the bauble shape you will need to adjust the number of A beads in the rods to accomodate the size variation in the bauble. Look at the length of the rods around the bauble and estimate the number of A beads you will need to add or subtract to make the rods the correct length so they meet neatly at the bottom of the bauble. Remove the needle from the thread and unpick the last row of loops. Work the row a second time with the A bead adjustment you have calculated to make a snugly-fitted net over the surface of the bauble.

**6** Run the needle around the ring of B beads at the bottom of the bauble a second time to make it secure. Now that the net fits snugly over the bauble shape you can add the remaining two rows of swags to the top part of the design.

Pass the needle up through one of the rods to emerge through the B bead at the top of the rod. Pass the needle up through the A bead to the left of the top B bead (fig 6).

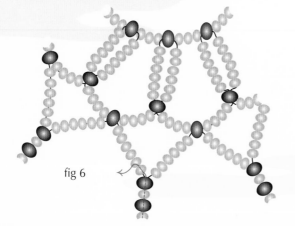

fig 6

**7** Thread on 1A. Pass the needle down through the A bead to the right of the B bead at the top of the rod (fig 7). Thread on 11A, 1B, 1A, 1C, 1B and 3A. Leaving aside the 3A beads to anchor the strand turn the needle and pass it back up through the last B bead, the following C bead, 1A and 1B. Thread on 11A. Pass the needle up through the A

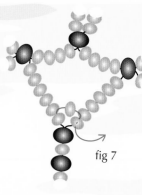

fig 7

bead to the left of the B bead at the top of the next rod around the net (fig 8). Repeat right around the bauble to add a further six C bead swags finishing with the needle emerging through the A bead to the left of the B bead at the top of the first rod.

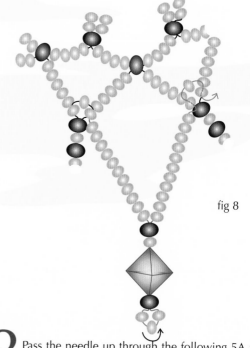

fig 8

**8** Pass the needle up through the following 5A and 1B beads to emerge with the needle pointing to the left through the B bead at the bottom of the first row of netting (fig 9).

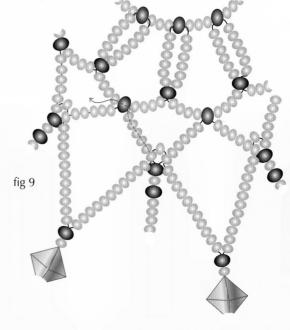

fig 9

# 9

Thread on 7A, 1B, 1D, 1B and 7A. Pass the needle through the B bead at the bottom of the first row once more to bring the beads just threaded into a hanging loop below the B bead (fig 10) - do not pull the thread too tightly or the loop will stand proud of the bauble: just allow enough slack in the thread so the loop falls softly.

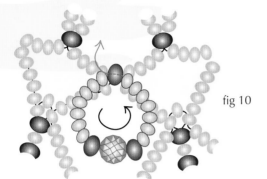

fig 10

# 10

Pass the needle up through the following 4A, 1B and 6A of the first row of netting to emerge through the B bead on the top ring made in step 1 (fig 11). Now pass the needle down through the 6A, 1B, 4A and 1B of the next loop on the first row of netting to be in the correct position to add the next hanging loop of 7A, 1B, 1D, 1B and 7A.

Repeat steps 9 and 10 right around the bauble to add a full complement of seven hanging loops.

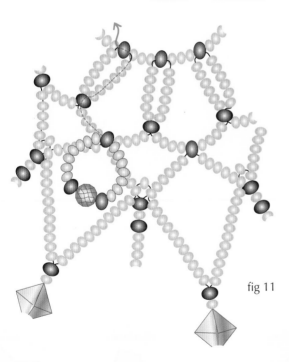

fig 11

If you have 1m of thread remaining work the needle down through the beads of the bauble net to emerge through one of the B beads of the ring of 7B at the very bottom of the bauble. If you do not have sufficient thread remaining finish off this end neatly and start a new thread to emerge through one of the B beads at the bottom of the bauble.

# 11

The Tassel Strand - The bottom tassel strand is supported by the B beads of the ring - it will hang across the space in the centre. Thread on 4A, 1B, 1D, 1B, 1A, 1C, 1B, 4A, 1D, 4A, 1B, 1E, 1B, 1A, 1B, 1C, 1B, 1D, 1B and 3A. Leaving aside the last 3A threaded to anchor the strand pass the needle back up through the last B bead threaded and the following 1D, 1B, 1C, 1B, 1A, 1B, 1E and 1B. Thread on 4A, 1D and 4A. Pass the needle back up though the next B bead of the strand and the following 1C, 1A, 1B, 1D and 1B. Thread on 4A (fig 12).

# 12

Referring to fig 13 the tassel strand was begun after emerging from bead W on the ring of 7B. Pass the needle through bead Y of the ring and through the following 2B to emerge through bead Z on fig 13. Tension the thread so that the tassel strand hangs softly from below the bauble with no loops of thread showing between the beads.

The strand is now enhanced with one more pass of the thread.

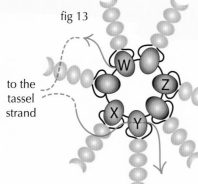

fig 13

to the tassel strand

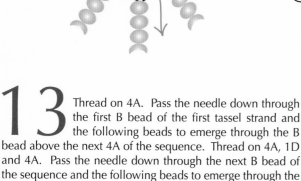

fig 12

# 13

Thread on 4A. Pass the needle down through the first B bead of the first tassel strand and the following beads to emerge through the B bead above the next 4A of the sequence. Thread on 4A, 1D and 4A. Pass the needle down through the next B bead of the sequence and the following beads to emerge through the bottom A bead of the anchor. Passing the needle through the remaining bead of the anchor bring the needle back up through the tassel strand beads to emerge through the B bead immediately above the E bead.

# 14

Thread on 4A, 1D and 4A. Pass the needle up through the next B bead of the tassel strand to emerge through the top B bead of the sequence. Thread on 4A.

Pass the needle through the X bead on fig 13 to centralise the tassel strand below the bauble. Tension the thread if necessary and finish off the thread end securely.

# 15

The Hanging Loop - Prepare the needle with 75cm of doubled thread and tie on a keeper bead 15cm from the end.

Thread on 1D, 1B, 1C, 1B and 1E. Pass the needle through the metal loop at the top of the bauble and back up through the beads just threaded (fig 14).

Thread on 1B and 3A ten times to make the hanging loop (add more repeats if you need a longer loop). Pass the needle down through the 1B above the D bead to emerge alongside the keeper bead.

Remove the keeper bead and tie the ends of the thread to the needle end of the thread securely. Pass both ends of the thread through a few beads before trimming to make a neat finish to the work.

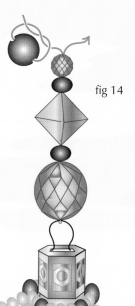

fig 14

# Art Deco Inspirations

The Art Deco design will scale up for larger sizes of baubles quite easily but the central tassel strand can look a little narrow on a 40mm or 60mm bauble. Try making the tassel strand a little longer or substituting it with a full tassel as made in the Net & Tassel design on page 29. Alternatively you can take elements of the bead sequence to create a new design as below.

## This Design is Worked Over a 40mm Bauble

### You Will Need
8g of size 10/0 silver lined gold seed beads A
3g of size 8/0 silver lined purple AB seed beads B
One 6mm topaz AB fire polished facet C
Twenty-seven 4mm purple AB fire polished beads D
One 6mm purple AB fire polished faceted bead E

**1** Follow step 1 from the main instructions for the Art Deco design on page 21.

**2** Work steps 2 and 3 from the main instructions as before but with a count of 10A, 1B, 7A, 1B, 7A, 1B and 10A.

**3** Thread on 10A, 1B and 10A and pass through the bottom B bead on the next loop around the bauble. Thread on 5A, 1B, 1A, 1D, 1A, 1B and 5A. Pass the needle through the same B bead on the bottom of the loop in the same direction as before to make a small circular dangling loop (as fig 10).

Repeat this step around the bauble. Bring the needle through the first 10A and 1B of the first swag ready to begin the next step.

**4** Thread on 12A, 1B, 5A, 1B, 4A, 1B, 1A, 1D, 1A, 1B and 4A. Pass the needle through the second B bead just added in the same direction as before to draw up the small circular loop of beads.

fig 15

Pass the needle back up the following 5A and 1B in the opposite direction to the one before and thread on 12A. Pass the needle through the B bead at the bottom of the next swag around the bauble (fig 15).

**5** Thread on 5A, 1B, 1A, 1D, 1A, 1B and 5A. Make a small circular loop by passing the needle through the B bead on the bottom of the swag in the same direction as before (as fig 10). Repeat the last two steps around the bauble and finish off the thread ends.

**6** The hanging loop is made with a circle of six repeats of 1A, 1D which are pulled up into the circle by passing the needle through the beads a second time.

Reposition the needle to emerge through an A bead and thread on 1A, 1B and 1A. Pass the needle through the loop at the top of the bauble and back up through the beads just added to the edge of the circle. Pass the needle through the A bead on the circle in the same direction as before.

Pass the needle across the centre of the bead circle adding 1A, 1C and 1A. Pass the needle through the A bead on the opposite side of the circle.

Finish off the sequence above the circle with 1A, 1B, 1A, 1E, 1A, 1B and sufficient A beads to make the loop to the required size (fig 16).

fig 16

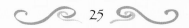

# Net & Tassel Bauble

## You Will Need

### Materials

One 40mm frosted red glass bauble
6g of size 10/0 silver lined gold seed beads A
3g of size 8/0 silver lined red seed beads B
2.5g of size 3 silver lined red bugle beads C
Ten red 6mm fire polished faceted beads D
One red 8mm fire polished faceted bead E
One red 12mm fire polished faceted bead F
Two 4mm gilt jump rings
One 8mm gilt filigree beadcup
Two 5mm gilt filigree beadcups
A reel of red size D beading thread

### Tools

A size 10 beading needle
A pair of scissors to trim the threads
A pair of fine pliers to open and close the jump ring

The netted beadwork that covers the bauble needs to fit quite snugly over the 40mm bauble shape. As the bead sizes vary very slightly and bauble diameters are not always precise you may need to make a little adjustment in the bead count to make the net fit properly. Guidance is given for this adjustment when necessary. This design uses a quick and easy method for making tassels - see the extra inspirations at the end of the chapter and you will soon have tassels attached to everything!

The Decoration is Made in Four Stages
The foundation row around the neck.
The tightly fitted net that covers the bauble.
The tassel which links onto the bottom of the net.
The hanging loop at the top of the bauble.

**1** The Foundation Row - Prepare the needle with 2.5m of single thread. Tie a keeper bead 15cm from the end. Thread seven repeats of 3A and 1B. Drape the beads around the neck of the bauble to form a ring.

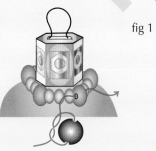

fig 1

**2** Check the fit of the beads around the bauble neck - it needs to be quite tight but with no thread showing between the beads - if necessary you can adjust the bead count to 2A and 1B or up to 4A and 1B - you just need the 7B beads to be evenly spaced around the neck of the bauble. When you are happy with the fit pass the needle through the beads a second time to draw the beads up into a ring bringing the needle to emerge from the first B bead threaded (fig 1). This completes the foundation row from which the remainder of the design will hang.

**3** The Netting - Thread on 5A, 1B, 5A, 1B, 5A, 1B and 5A to make the first loop of the pattern. Pass the needle through the next B bead around the foundation row (fig 2).

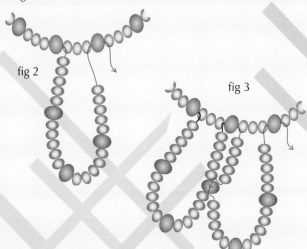

fig 2

fig 3

**4** Thread on 5A. Pass the needle down through the last B bead of the previous loop and thread on 5A, 1B, 5A, 1B and 5A. Pass the needle through the next B bead around the foundation row (fig 3).

**5** Repeat step 4 four more times. The final loop of the row needs to connect the last loop and the first loop made. Thread on 5A. Pass the needle down through the last B bead of the last loop; thread on 5A, 1B and 5A. Pass the needle up through the first B bead of the first loop and thread on 5A. Finish the loop by passing the needle through the next B bead on the foundation row (fig 4).

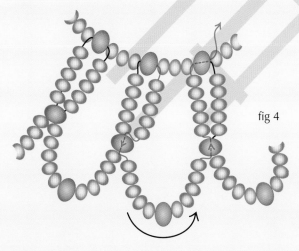

fig 4

**6** Before beginning the next row of netting the needle needs to be repositioned. Pass the needle down through the 5A, 1B, 5A and 1B to emerge through the centre bottom bead of the first loop of row one (fig 5). The next row hangs from this centre bead B on each of the first row loops.

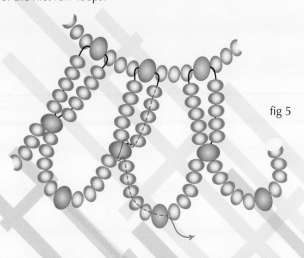

fig 5

### Extra Info....
This design uses bead filigree cups to enhance the large faceted bead underneath the bauble and to bring together the strands of the attached tassel. Bead cups can just be used decoratively, as in this design, but if you have beads with unevenly shaped or impractically large holes try using bead cups to even out the differences - they can work wonders.

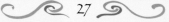

**7** This next row will complete the netted part of the design adding the large F bead at the bottom of the bauble. The large F bead needs to hang centrally at the bottom of the bauble.

Adjusting to Fit - The bead count of 21A above the F bead in step 8 should bring the F bead into the correct position, but bead sizes, and bauble sizes, can vary a little. To compensate you may need to alter the bead count of 21A slightly. Work through steps 8 and 9 as stated and then examine the fit of the beading to the bauble. The F bead needs to hang vertically from the bottom of the bauble so make sure the beading is neither too tight nor too loose. If necessary remove the needle and unpick the work so you can adjust the count of 21A. Use this same A bead count on all of the bead straps supporting the F bead.

**8** Thread on 5A, 1B, 21A, 1B, one small beadcup, 1F and the second small beadcup so that the two beadcups enclose either end of the larger facet bead. Pass the needle through one of the jump rings and back up through most of the beads just added to emerge at the top of the 21A beads. Pass the needle through the B bead above the 21A in the same direction as before (fig 6).

fig 6

**9** Thread on 5A. Pass the needle through the central B bead of the next loop on the first row (fig 7).

With reference to step 7 above check the fit of the netting around the bauble and make any neccessary adjustments to the count of 21A.

fig 7

**10** Thread on 5A, 1B and the correct number of A beads to reach the B bead above the F bead. Pass the needle down through the 1B, the top beadcup, 1F, the bottom beadcup and the jump ring. Pass the needle back up through the bottom beadcup, 1F, the top beadcup and the 1B. Pass the needle up through the long strand of A beads just added to emerge just below the first B bead of this step. Pass the needle through the B bead as in fig 6 and thread on 5A. Pass the needle through the central B bead of the next loop of the first row (as fig 7).

Repeat step 10 until you have worked right around the bauble. Check the fit of the netting around the bauble - if all is satisfactory finish off the thread end securely.

Return to the keeper bead from step 1. Remove the keeper and finish off this end of the thread securely.

**11** The Tassel - Prepare the needle with 2.5m of single thread and tie a keeper bead 15cm from the end. Thread on 1B. Pass the needle through the large filigree beadcup from the outside to the inside of the cup shape. Thread on 20A, 1C, 6A, 1B, 1A, 1C, 1A, 2B, 4A, 1B, 1D, 1B, 1A, 1B and 7A. Leaving aside the 7A just added pass the needle back up through all of the remaining beads to emerge at the keeper bead at the top of the strand. Pass the needle through a new jump ring (fig 8).

fig 8

**12** Untie the keeper bead at the start of the thread. Carefully tie this thread end to the needle end pulling the knot down firmly to the top B bead trapping the jump ring snugly against the bead - do not pull too tightly or the tassel strand will be rigid - leave just a little give in the thread so the tassel strand falls softly.

Adjust the jump ring so that the thread loop cannot sneek through the gap in the ring.

fig 9

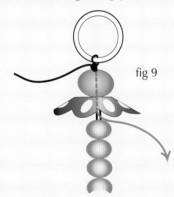

**13** Pass the needle back down through the top B bead and the filigree beadcup ready to start the next tassel strand (fig 9). Thread on 20A, 1C, 6A, 1B, 1A, 1C, 1A, 2B, 4A, 1B, 1D, 1B, 1A, 1B and 7A.

Make the strand as before, passing the needle up through the filigree cup and the B bead above it. Pass the needle through the jump ring and back down the B bead and the filigree beadcup to start the third strand.

Make nine strands in total in the same manner.

**14** Knot the remaining thread onto the thread end from the beginning of the tassel. Pass the needle down through the beads of one of the tassel strands to neaten before trimming. Return to the other thread end. Attach the needle to this end of the thread and neaten in an identical manner before trimming.

Open either the jump ring attached to the bottom of the bauble or the ring at the top of the tassel and link the two parts of the decoration together.

**15** The Hanging Loop - To complete the decoration you will need to add the beaded hanging loop to the top of the bauble.

Prepare the needle with 75cm of doubled thread and tie a keeper bead 15cm from the ends. Thread on 1D, 1B, 1A, 1B, 1E, 1B and 1A. Pass the needle through the loop at the top of the bauble and back up through the beads just threaded (fig 10).

fig 10

Thread on 1A, 2B, 1A, 1B, 36A, 1B, 1A and 2B to make the loop (if you require a longer loop increase the count of 36A). Pass the needle back down the A bead above the D bead to bring the two sets of thread ends together.

Untie the keeper bead and tie the two sets of ends together securely. Neaten both sets of ends by passing back through several adjacent beads before trimming neatly.

# Tassel Inspirations

The tassel method used in the Net & Tassel bauble design is quick and easy. You can copy the technique to make plain tassels to decorate the tree or adapt it slightly to convert the tassels into key charms, pendants, bag charms, earrings or the final flourish to a cushion or light pull.

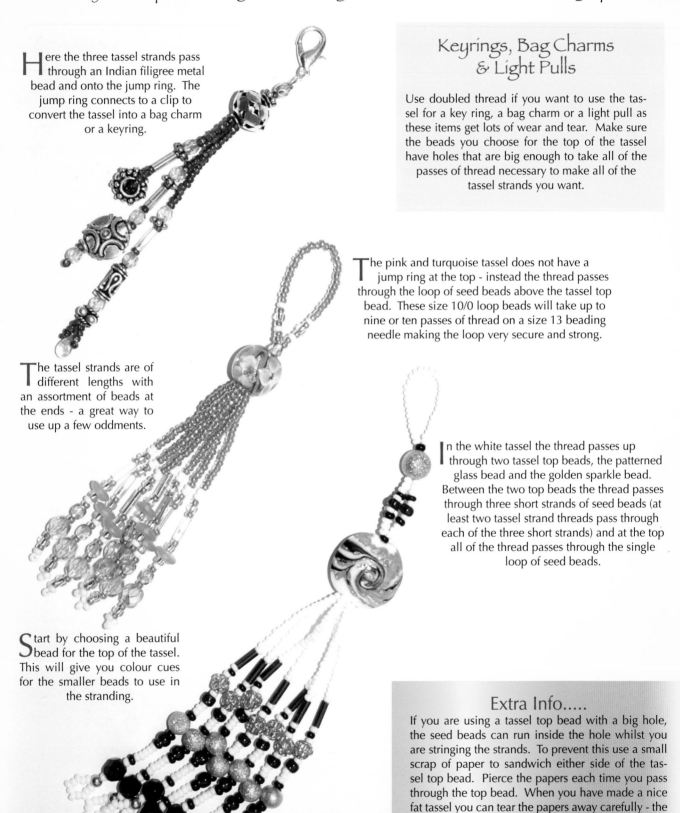

Here the three tassel strands pass through an Indian filigree metal bead and onto the jump ring. The jump ring connects to a clip to convert the tassel into a bag charm or a keyring.

The tassel strands are of different lengths with an assortment of beads at the ends - a great way to use up a few oddments.

Start by choosing a beautiful bead for the top of the tassel. This will give you colour cues for the smaller beads to use in the stranding.

## Keyrings, Bag Charms & Light Pulls

Use doubled thread if you want to use the tassel for a key ring, a bag charm or a light pull as these items get lots of wear and tear. Make sure the beads you choose for the top of the tassel have holes that are big enough to take all of the passes of thread necessary to make all of the tassel strands you want.

The pink and turquoise tassel does not have a jump ring at the top - instead the thread passes through the loop of seed beads above the tassel top bead. These size 10/0 loop beads will take up to nine or ten passes of thread on a size 13 beading needle making the loop very secure and strong.

In the white tassel the thread passes up through two tassel top beads, the patterned glass bead and the golden sparkle bead. Between the two top beads the thread passes through three short strands of seed beads (at least two tassel strand threads pass through each of the three short strands) and at the top all of the thread passes through the single loop of seed beads.

## Extra Info.....

If you are using a tassel top bead with a big hole, the seed beads can run inside the hole whilst you are stringing the strands. To prevent this use a small scrap of paper to sandwich either side of the tassel top bead. Pierce the papers each time you pass through the top bead. When you have made a nice fat tassel you can tear the papers away carefully - the overall bulkiness of the tasssel strands will stop the top seed beads from sneaking up into the large hole of the tassel top bead.

# Shooting Star Tassel

You may recognise the shape and form of the top star from the Sirius Star chapter (page 17) and the dangling stars from the Starry Night chapter (page 50). If you have made both of these star shapes already you will find this Shooting Star design very easy to make.

## You Will Need
Fifteen 6mm crystal AB fire polished faceted beads A
4g of size 8/0 silver lined gold seed beads B
3g of size 3 silver lined gold bugle beads C
5g of size 10/0 silver lined gold seed beads D
One 12mm crystal AB fire polished faceted bead E
One 8mm crystal AB fire polished faceted bead F
Four 4mm crystal AB fire polished faceted beads G
Two 4mm gold plated jump rings
A reel of white size D beading thread

1 The Sirius Star - Make the top star as in the Sirius Star chapter (page 17) but note in this recipe you are using 6mm fire polished facets as A instead of 4mm crystal and size 8/0 seed beads as B instead of size 10/0 seed beads. Use a single thickness of thread to work the star as in the Sirius Star chapter but pass the needle through each stitch a second time to make the beading stronger and more firm. Do not finish off the thread.

2 The Connection for the Tassel - Pass the needle through the work to emerge through the closest A bead of the ring made in steps 1-4 of the Sirius Star instructions. Thread on 4D, 1B, 8D, 1G and a jump ring. Pass the needle back up the 1G, 8D and 1B beads. Thread on 4D and pass the needle through the A bead on the Sirius Star in the same direction as before (fig 11).

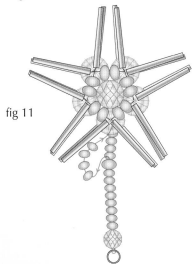

fig 11

3 The Hanging Loop - Bring the needle through the work to emerge through the B bead at the tip of the star point immediately opposite the position of the tassel connector just made in step 2. Thread on 5D, 1B, 1E, 1B and 45D. Pass the needle back down the 1B, 1E, 1B and 5D to draw up the loop. Pass the needle through the B bead at the tip of the star in the same direction as before and finish off the thread end securely.

4 The Tassel - Start the tassel as for the Net & Tassel Bauble on page 29 with a jump ring. Thread on 1F and 1B for the tassel top. Thread on 10D, 1C, 2D and 1G. Make a Fringe Star as described on page 51 (steps 4, 5 and 6) with D and B beads. Add the dangle at the bottom of the fringe star with 1C, 1D, 1B, 1A, 1B and 1D instead of the combination stated in the Starry Night chapter.

When you have completed the Fringe Star pass the needle back up to the top of the tassel strand beads to emerge at the jump ring. Make the next tassel strand with 20D above the C bead and the third tassel strand with 30D above the C bead.

Finish off all the thread ends and link the two jump rings together to complete the design.

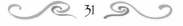

# Aragon Bauble

## You Will Need

### Materials

One 40mm frosted silver glass bauble
2g of size 8/0 silver lined crystal seed beads A
10g of size 10/0 silver lined crystal seed beads B
8g of size 10/0 frosted crystal seed beads C
2g of size 3 silver lined crystal bugle beads D
Twenty-one 4mm crystal fire polished faceted beads E
Nine 6mm crystal fire polished faceted beads F
One 10mm crystal fire polished faceted bead G
A reel of white size D beading thread

### Tools

A size 13 beading needle
A pair of scissors to trim the threads

The Tudor headdresses and rows of beads strung across the flat fronted bodices of Court attire in 16th century England inspired this elegant design. It brings together several simple techniques which build into the final decoration - it is easy to adapt for different size bauble ornaments - see page 37.

The Decoration is Made in Five Stages
First you make the foundation row.
Then trumpet-shaped cones that support the tassels.
The tassels which pull up into the cones are next.
Followed by the swags in-between the cones.
The hanging loop completes the decoration.

**1** The Foundation Row - Prepare the needle with 1.8m of single thread and tie a keeper bead 15cm from the end. Thread on 1A, 9B, 1A, 9B, 1A and 9B. Drape the beads around the neck of the bauble. If the beads do not meet together try with 8B or 10B between the A beads until you get a snug fit - you need the three single A beads spaced evenly around the neck of the bauble. Pass the needle through the beads a second time to form a ring. Bring the needle out through the first A bead of the ring (fig 1) in the correct position to start the cones.

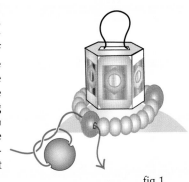

fig 1

**2** The Cones - you will work on one cone at a time. The three cones hang from the 3A beads of the ring. Thread on 2B, 1A and 2B. Pass the needle through the A bead on the ring in the same direction as before and through the following 2B and 1A just added (fig 2).

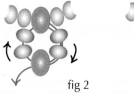 

fig 2          fig 3

**3** Thread on 2B. Pass the needle through the A bead of the previous stitch in the same direction as before and the 2B just added (fig 3).

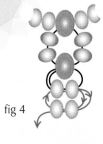 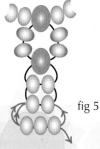

fig 4          fig 5

Thread on 2B. Pass the needle through the 2B beads of the previous row and the 2B just added (fig 4) to bring the two rows parallel to one another.

Thread on 3B. Pass the needle through the 2B beads of the previous stitch and the 3B beads just added (fig 5). This ladder stitch technique builds up the bottom layer of the cone.

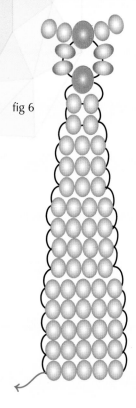

fig 6

**4** Fig 6 shows all the rows of the bottom layer of the cone. Starting with another two rows of 3B beads each, work down the rows as shown in fig 6 to complete the pattern down to the bottom row of the layer. Leave the needle emerging from the end of the last row (fig 6).

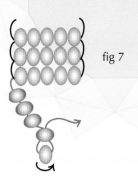

fig 7

**5** Thread on 5B. Leaving aside the last B bead threaded to anchor the strand pass the needle back up through the fourth B bead just added (fig 7). Thread on 3B and pass the needle through the last row of 5B in the same direction as before (fig 8). This little point on the end of the bottom row of the cone will keep the last row worked in fig 6 straight.

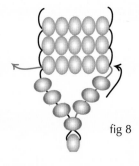

fig 8

**6** The bottom layer of the cone is now used to support the beaded loops that make up the curved front of the cones. Thread on 15C. Pass the needle through the last row of 5B beads (fig 9) to bring the new beads into a loop to the front of the row.
Pass the needle back through the 5B beads of the row above this one (fig 10).

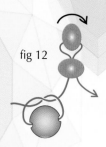

fig 12

**9** The Tassels - Prepare the needle with 1.2m of single thread and tie on a keeper bead 15cm from the end. Thread on 2A. Turn the needle and pass back through the first A bead threaded in the opposite direction to draw the second A bead into an anchor (fig 12) - this will be the top of the tassel.

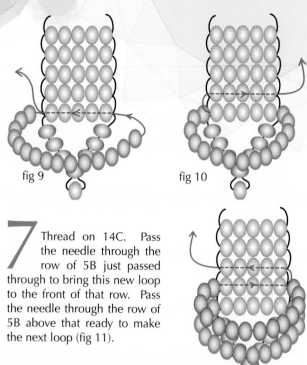

fig 9        fig 10

fig 11

**7** Thread on 14C. Pass the needle through the row of 5B just passed through to bring this new loop to the front of that row. Pass the needle through the row of 5B above that ready to make the next loop (fig 11).

**10** Following fig 13 thread on the beads for the first strand on the tassel - 30B, 1C, 5B, 2C, 4B, 3C, 3B, 4C, 2B, 5C, 1D, 1C, 1A, 1C, 1D, 1C, 1A, 1C, 1F, 1C, 1E and 1C. Turn the needle and leaving the last C bead threaded to anchor the strand pass the needle back up through the E bead and the following beads to emerge through the A bead right at the top of the strand (fig 13).

This A bead at the top allows you to turn the needle for the next strand - pass the needle through the A bead below it ready to start the new strand.

**8** Work up the remainder of the bottom layer adding 13C to this row; 12C to the one above that; 11C to the next and 10C to the next - work up to the top row of 2B where you will have reduced the count down to 2C beads. Work this loop of 2C.

If you have sufficient thread to start the next cone around the ring made in step 1 then work the needle through the A bead above the last row worked; the 2B beads that connect to the ring and through the A and B beads of the ring to emerge through the next A bead around the ring ready to begin the next cone.

If you do not have sufficient thread to start the next cone leave the thread end loose without knotting off and start a new thread for the next cone. Do not knot off the threads between the beads of the cones yet - the needle needs to pass through these beads again and any knots may block the holes.

Work the remaining two cones around the ring following steps 2 to 8 inclusive.

**11** Start this strand with 24B instead of 30B but follow the remainder of the sequence as in fig 13. Turn the needle at the bottom of the strand and pass right back up to emerge through the A bead at the very top (as fig 13).

Pass the needle back down the A bead below this top A bead ready to start the third tassel strand. Start this tassel strand with 16B instead of 30B but make the remainder of the strand as before bringing the needle up to the top of the tassel through the top A bead.

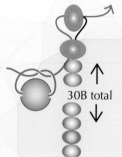

30B total

fig 13

**12** Remove the needle from this end of the thread and untie the keeper bead. Reattach the needle to this end of the thread and finish off the end neatly without blocking the hole in the top A bead of the tassel. Trim this thread end only.

Reattach the needle to the other end of the thread - this end is now used to attach the tassel inside the cone.

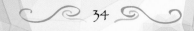

**13** Fig 14 shows the back of the first cone with the beads that will support the top of the tassel shown in purple. Pass the needle at the top of the tassel up through the hollow cone shape between the bottom layer made in fig 6 and the loops made in steps 6, 7 and 8. It is quite a tight fit but pull the needle through to emerge between the first two rows of 4B beads at the back of the cone. Pass the needle through the two beads marked in purple on fig 16 and through the A bead at the top of the tassel once more - this is a little awkward as you will have to dig the needle between the rows of B beads at the back of the cone but try to pull the thread tightly to draw the top of the tassel into place.

If possible repeat the stitch to make the attachment more secure. Leave the thread end loose and repeat from the beginning of step 9 to make a further two tassels and attach them to the other two cones.

fig 14

**14** The Swags - Prepare the needle with 2m of single thread and tie a keeper bead 15cm from the end. Pass the needle through the beads of the ring made in step 1 and bring it down through the beads at the top of the first cone to emerge through the end of the first row of 2B as seen in fig 6. This is the position to start the first layer of swags which hang between the cones. Fig 15 shows the beads down the edges of the bottom layer of the cones that support the swags - at present the needle should be emerging through one of the beads marked in yellow.

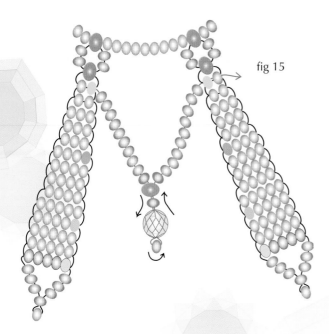

fig 15

**15** Thread on 9B, 1C, 1A, 1C, 1E and 1C. Turn the needle and pass it back up through the E bead and the following 1C and 1A (fig 15). Thread on 1C and 9B. Pass the needle through the corresponding row of 2B at the top of the bottom layer of the next cone around the bauble (fig 15) - note that the needle passes through the beads of the bottom layer and NOT the top looped layer of the cone.

**16** Repeat to add another swag with an identical bead count between this second cone and the third cone. Repeat to make a third swag to bring the needle back around to the first cone. Work the needle down through the rows of B beads on the bottom layer of the first cone to emerge through the edge of the first row of 4B (marked green in fig 15). You will need to make a swag here in a similar manner.

**17** Thread on 14B, 1C, 1A, 1C, 1E and 1C. Turn the needle as before to emerge through the top of the A bead and thread on 1C, 14B to complete the swag passing the needle through the first row of 4B on the next cone around (see green beads in fig 15). Work around the bauble to add another two swags to match.

**18** Work the needle down through the B beads of the bottom layer of the first cone to emerge through the end of the second row of 5B (blue in fig 15) to start the next row of swags. Make this row as for the last substituting the 14B bead count for 17B. Work three swags in total around the bauble.

Reposition the needle to emerge through one of the beads marked pink in fig 15 for the last row of swags. Start this row with 19B and make three swags around the bauble as before.

Finish off the thread end and all other remaining thread ends neatly.

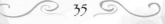

**19** The Hanging Loop - Prepare the needle with 1.2m of single thread and tie on a keeper bead 15cm from the end.

Thread on the large faceted bead G. Pass the needle through the metal loop at the top of the bauble and back up the faceted bead. Thread on 1A, 1C and 1A (fig 16).

fig 16

**20** Thread on sufficient C beads to make a hanging loop for your bauble (approximately 40C). Pass the needle back down through the A, C, A and the faceted bead to draw up the loop.

The faceted bead is now enhanced with a few straps of small seed beads. You will make four straps in total - you can alternate the straps to make two in C and two in B or make them all the same colour - the choice is yours. The instructions will assume that you are starting with B beads.

fig 17

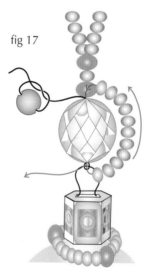

**21** Thread on 11B. Pass the needle down through the faceted bead once more to bring the B beads into a strap around the facet (fig 17). Check that a count of 11B is long enough to go around the facet - you may need to alter the bead count slightly - if you do need to alter the count remove the needle from the thread and pull the thread back through the facet before re-threading the needle - this will prevent the thread from splitting and fraying inside the facet.

When the bead count is correct repeat step 21 to add three more straps of seed beads to decorate the facet.

**22** Before finishing off the thread pass the needle through the metal loop at the top of the bauble and back up the facet to make the attachment to the bauble a little stronger. Finish off both ends of the thread securely.

## Aragon Inspiration

If you change the 40mm bauble for a 60mm bauble there is more room for cones and swags.

This 60mm bauble has five cones - each one is a little larger than on the 40mm bauble design.

To make the larger cones work fig 6 with 3 rows of 2B, 4 rows of 4B, five rows of 5B and seven rows of 6B. This forms a larger cone base so you will need to start the bead loops (as fig 9) to the front of the cones with 20C.

There are four swags between the cones and the tassel strands are longer to keep all of the proportions in order.

A graduated palette is used with silver lined gold, bronze and brown size 10/0 seed beads, scarab green size 8/0 seed beads and olive green AB fire polished facets.

# Georgian Bauble

## You Will Need

### Materials

One 40mm frosted lilac glass bauble
7g of size 10/0 silver lined crystal seed beads A
3g of size 8/0 silver lined purple seed beads B
3g of size 3 silver lined purple bugle beads C
Twenty-one 4mm purple fire polished faceted beads D
Thirteen 6mm purple fire polished faceted beads E
A reel of lilac size D beading thread

### Tools

A size 10 beading needle
A pair of scissors to trim the threads

*D*elicacy and femininity abounded in the quality furnishings of the Georgian Period. Explorers were in every corner of the world seeking out new delights and botanical specimens were flooding into Europe. Fine muslins for grand dresses were printed and embroidered with tiny flowers and blossoms which inspired this flower wreathed decoration.

The Decoration is Made in Three Stages
The foundation row around the neck of the bauble.
The flower garlands with the dangling strands.
The hanging loop for the top of the decoration.

**1** The Foundation Row - Prepare the needle with 1.8m of single thread. Thread on 5A, 1B, 5A, 1B, 5A, 1B, 5A and 1B. Tie the two ends of the thread together to draw the beads up into a secure ring leaving a tail of thread 15cm long. Drop the ring over the top of the bauble. Pass the needle through the first 5A and 1B beads of the ring (fig 1).

fig 1

**2** Thread on 1A, 1C and 1B. Pass the needle back up the C bead and thread on 1A. Pass the needle through the B bead on the ring in the same direction as before (fig 2).

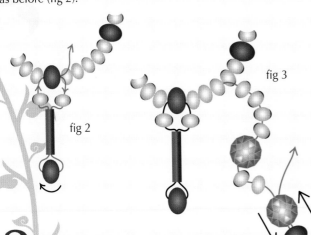

fig 2

fig 3

**3** Pass the needle through the next 3A of the ring and thread on 4A, 1D, 2A, 1D, 1B and 3A. Leaving aside the last 3A beads threaded to anchor the strand pass the needle back up through the 1B and 1D beads just threaded (fig 3).

**4** Thread on 2A and pass the needle through the top D bead in the opposite direction to the one before. Thread on 4A and pass the needle through the third A bead of the ring in the same direction as before (fig 4). Pass the needle through the following 2A and 1B of the ring.

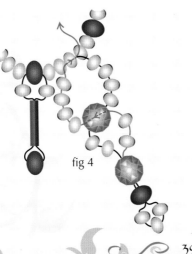

fig 4

**5** Repeat steps 2, 3 and 4 three more times to give four equally spaced pendants of two types around the ring. Bring the needle through the beads of the ring so that it emerges alongside the other end of the thread. Tie the needle end of the thread to the tail end to secure. Pass the needle through the next few beads of the design to neaten before trimming. Attach the needle to the tail end of the thread and neaten similarly. This completes the foundation row.

**6** The Flower Garlands - Prepare the needle with 2m of single thread. Tie a keeper bead 15cm from the end. Thread on 1D and 3B. Pass the needle through the D bead a second time to bring the 3B beads around the edge of the D bead (fig 5).

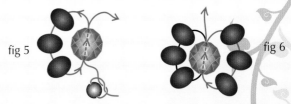

fig 5                                                                    fig 6

Thread on 3B and pass the needle through the D bead again to bring these beads around the opposite side of the D bead (fig 6). Pass the needle down through the second 3B added and thread on 1B. Pass the needle through the first 3B beads (fig 7). Thread on 1B and pass the needle through the next 4B beads of the sequence (fig 8).

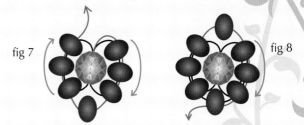

fig 7                                                                    fig 8

39

**7** Thread on 5A, 1B, 1A, 1B, 3A, 1E, 1B and 3A. Leaving aside the last 3A beads threaded to anchor the strand pass the needle back up the 1B, 1E and 1A beads (fig 9). Thread on 2A and pass the needle through the B bead above the 2A in the opposite direction to the one before and thread on 1A, 1B and 5A. Pass the needle through the B bead on the ring that you emerged from in the same direction as before (fig 10).

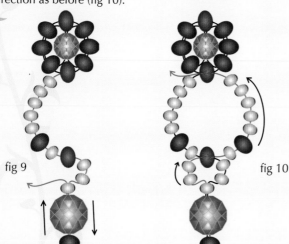

fig 9

fig 10

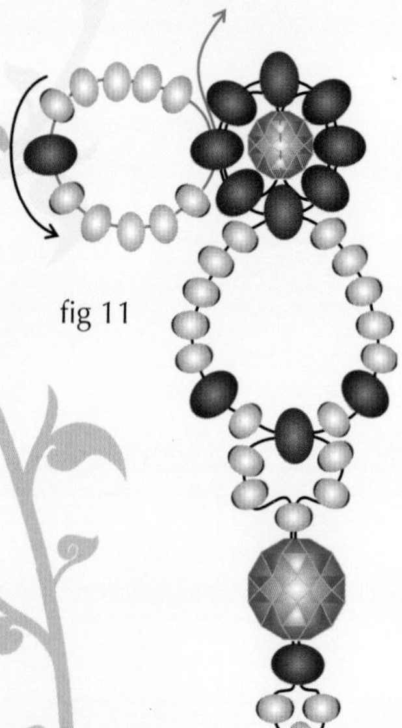

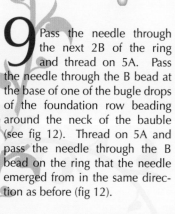

fig 11

**8** Pass the needle through the next 2B of the ring and thread on 5A, 1B and 5A. Pass the needle through the B bead on the ring in the same direction as before (fig 11).

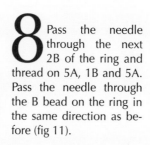

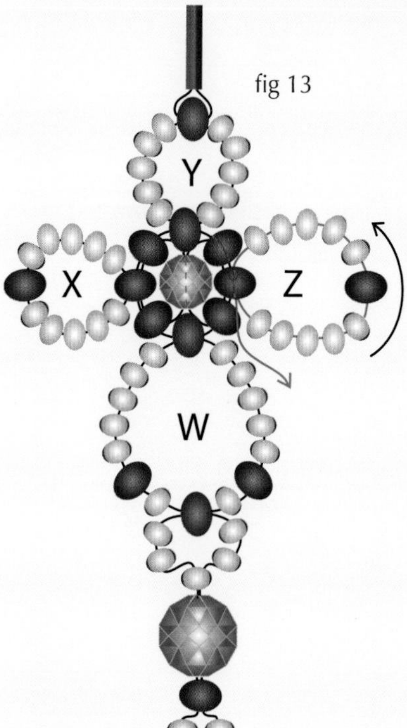

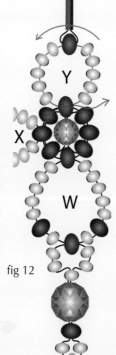

fig 12

**9** Pass the needle through the next 2B of the ring and thread on 5A. Pass the needle through the B bead at the base of one of the bugle drops of the foundation row beading around the neck of the bauble (see fig 12). Thread on 5A and pass the needle through the B bead on the ring that the needle emerged from in the same direction as before (fig 12).

fig 13

Y

X          Z

W

**10** Pass the needle through the next 2B of the ring and thread on 5A, 1B and 5A. Pass the needle through the B bead on the ring that you emerged from in the same direction as before (fig 13). You now have the four petals W, X, Y and Z of the first flower.

The next link is attached to the B bead of petal Z. Pass the needle through the first 5A and 1B of petal Z ready to start the next step.

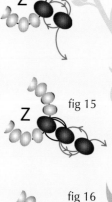

fig 14

Z

fig 15

Z

**11** Thread on 1B. Pass the needle back up through the B bead of the petal and back down the new B bead (fig 14) - this is ladder stitch. Thread on 1B and pass the needle back down the previous B bead and back up the new B bead (fig 15). Thread on 1A, 1B, 1A, 1E and 1A. Pass the needle back up the B bead the needle emerged from (fig 16).

fig 16

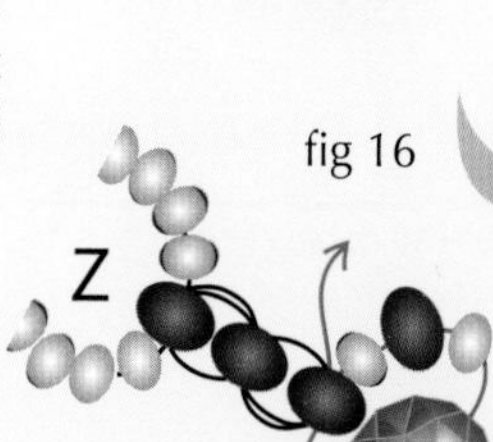

Z

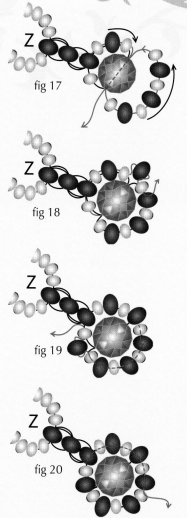
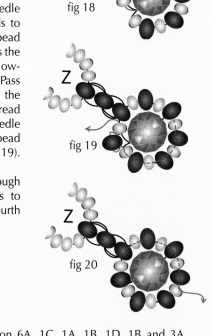

**12** Pass the needle through the following 1A, 1B and 1A beads and the E bead.

Thread on 1A, 1B, 1A, 1B, 1A, 1B and 1A. Pass the needle through the E bead (fig 17). Pass the needle through the five beads to the first side of the E bead and thread on 1B. Pass the needle through the following A bead (fig 18). Pass the needle through the next six beads and thread on 1B. Pass the needle through the next A bead around the E bead (fig 19).

Pass the needle through the next seven beads to emerge through the fourth B bead (fig 20).

fig 17

fig 18

fig 19

fig 20

fig 21

fig 22

fig 23

**13** Thread on 6A, 1C, 1A, 1B, 1D, 1B and 3A. Turn the needle and pass it back up through the bottom B bead and the following nine beads to emerge just below the first A bead of the strand. Thread on 1A and pass the needle through the next B bead around the ring (fig 21).

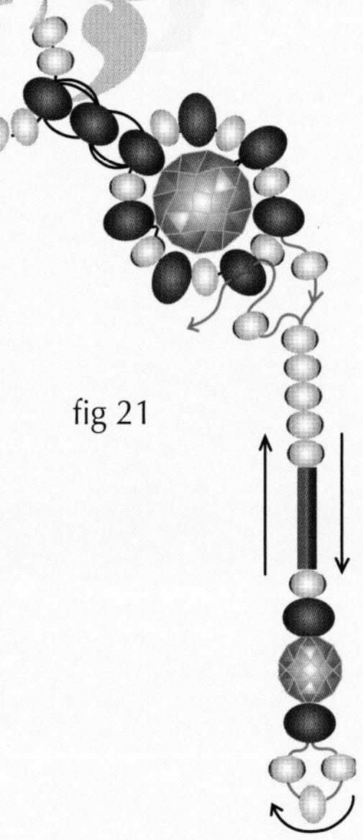

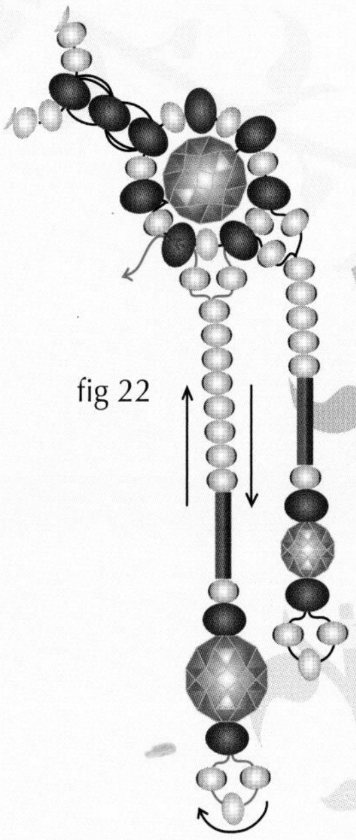

**14** Thread on 9A, 1C, 1A, 1B, 1E, 1B and 3A. Leaving aside the last 3A beads threaded to anchor the strand pass the needle back up through the bottom B bead and the following twelve beads to emerge just below the first A bead of the strand. Thread on 1A and pass the needle through the next B bead around the ring (fig 22).

Repeat step 13 to give three strands in total (fig 23).

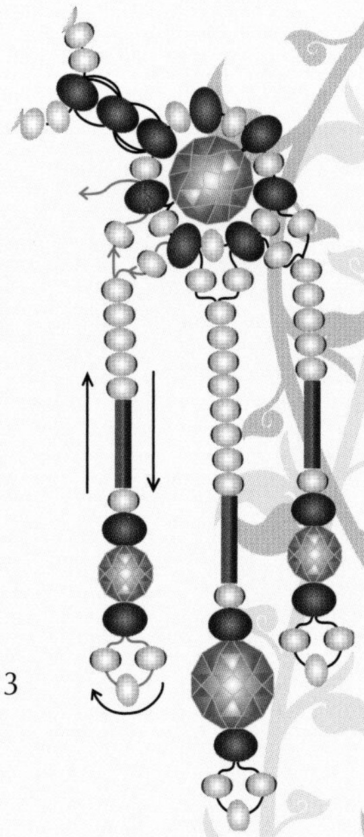

# Georgian Inspirations

The flower garland motifs will readily convert into delicate earrings and necklace designs.

The earrings use one complete circle around an E bead and the associated strands as in fig 23. To extend the length a few extra beads are added to the top of the circle.

A jump ring is required at the top of the design to ensure that the earring will swing properly when connected to the earfitting.

The necklace uses three E bead circles. The central circle is the same as fig 23 above. To make the design taper out to the sides a little the two circles to either side of the centre have two shorter dangling strands only.

The circles are linked together with tiny circles of A and B beads. The full neck length is made up with a simple repeat of an A and B bead sequence and finished with a bead tag and loop fastener (see page 56).

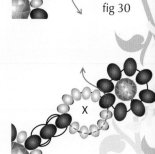

# 18

Thread on 5A. Pass the needle through the end B bead attached to the previous motif (fig 30) and back up the following 5A and 1B of the new petal (fig 31) - this completes the X petal of this flower motif.

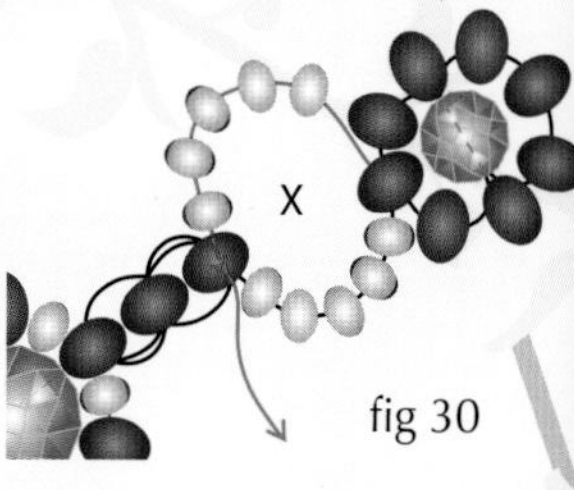

fig 30

fig 31

Pass the needle through the next 2B of the ring and make the Y petal to the top of the motif. Do not forget to pick up the B bead at the bottom of the next bugle pendant of the foundation row as the middle B bead of the petal. At the end of the Y petal move on to make the Z petal and the W petal as before (refer to fig 13 to see a complete motif).

# 15

Pass the needle through the next six beads of the ring to emerge through the third B bead of the ring. Thread on 1B and pass the needle back down the B bead on the ring. Pass the needle back up the new B bead (fig 24). Thread on 1B and repeat (fig 25).

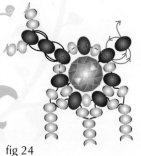

fig 24

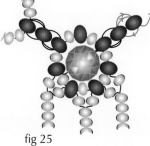

fig 25

# 19

After completing the second flower motif pass the needle through to emerge from the middle B bead of the Z petal and repeat steps 11, 12, 13 and 14 to make the second set of pendant strands followed by steps 15, 16, 17 and 18 to complete the third flower.

Repeat steps 11 to 18 to make the third set of pendant strands and the fourth flower.

Repeat steps 11 to 14 to make the last set of pendant strands.

This last set of pendant strands needs to be joined onto the middle B bead of the X petal of the first flower.

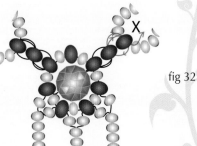

fig 32

# 16

Thread on 5A, 2B, 1D and 1B (fig 26). Pass the needle through the first 2B just added and back through the D bead to bring the 3B beads around the D bead (fig 27). Thread on 3B and pass the needle through the D bead again (fig 28). This D bead will be the centre of the next flower motif.

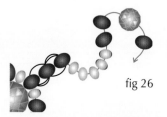

fig 26

fig 27

fig 28

# 17

Pass the needle through the first 3B added and thread on 1B. Pass the needle through the second 3B. Thread on 1B and pass the needle through the next 2B of the ring (fig 29).

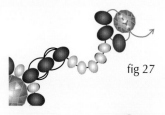

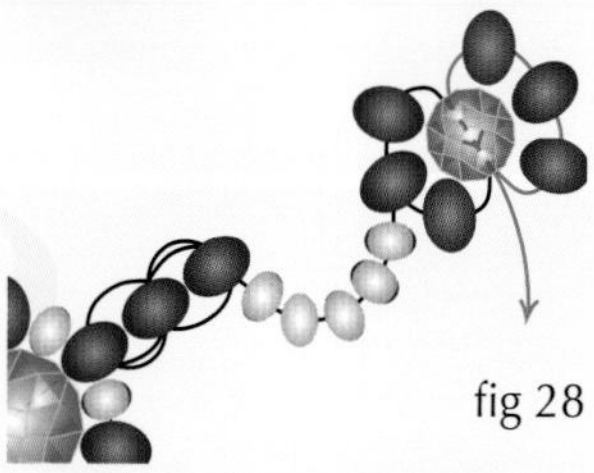

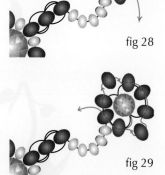

fig 29

# 20

Pass the needle around the ring to emerge through the third B bead of the ring as before. Thread on 1B and join onto the B bead of the ring as before. Pass the needle down through the middle B bead of the X petal on the first flower motif and up through the B bead just added. Pass the needle through the B bead of the petal once more to strengthen the link (fig 32).

Fasten off the thread end and neaten as before. Return to and remove the keeper bead. Fasten off this end of the thread and neaten similarly.

## Extra Info....
If the thread gets a little knotty and caught up on itself use a thread conditioner. Apply the conditioner after you have untangled the thread - it smooths the fibres back down and helps to prevent it reknotting and tangling in the same place again.

# 21

The Hanging Loop - Prepare the needle with 1.2m of single thread and tie a keeper bead 15cm from the end.

Thread on 1E, 1A, 1B, 1A, 1B, 1A, 1B and 1A. Pass the needle through the E bead (fig 33).

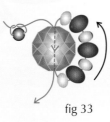

fig 33

# 22

Thread on 1A, 1B, 1A, 1B, 1A, 1B and 1A. Pass the needle through the E bead again (fig 34). Pass the needle through the second set of seven beads threaded and thread on 1B. Pass the needle through the following A bead (fig 35).

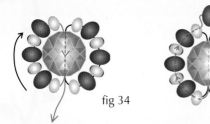

fig 34          fig 35

Pass the needle down the next six beads and thread on 1B. Pass the needle through the next A bead (fig 36).

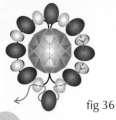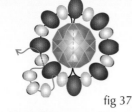

fig 36          fig 37

# 23

Thread on 3A and pass the needle through the next A bead of the ring around the E bead (fig 37). Repeat the last stitch twice.

Thread on 1A, 1B, 1D and 1B (fig 38). Thread on 45A to make the loop and pass the needle down the last 1B, 1D and 1B. Thread on 1A and pass the needle through the next A bead around the ring of beads (fig 39).

Repeat the first stitch of step 23 three more times.

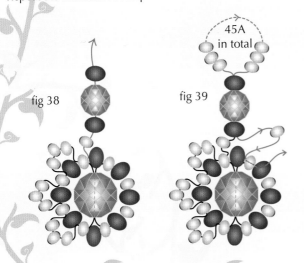

fig 38          fig 39

45A in total

# 24

Thread on 1A and 1B. Pass the needle through the metal loop at the top of the bauble. Pass the needle back up the B bead and thread on 1A. Pass the needle through the next A bead around the ring (fig 40).

Fasten off the thread as before.

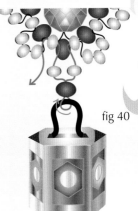

fig 40

# Swags & Tails Bauble

## You Will Need

### Materials

One 60mm frosted lilac glass bauble
10g of size 10/0 silver lined crystal seed beads A
10g of size 8/0 silver lined purple seed beads B
3g of size 3 AB purple bugle beads C
Thirteen 6mm purple fire polished faceted beads D
One 12mm purple fire polished faceted bead E
A reel of lilac size D beading thread

### Tools

A size 10 beading needle
A pair of scissors to trim the threads

The Swags & Tails design evokes a Victorian interior scene with ornate textiles and glittering crystal chandeliers. Made in rich reds or green with gold you are whisked back to Dickensian London - here we have used lilac and sparkling silver for a modern interpretation to hang on a white tree or a silver twig.

The Decoration is Made in Four Stages
The foundation row around the neck of the bauble.
The netted swags over the top half of the bauble.
The layered swags and tails that form the skirt.
The hanging loop.

**1** The Foundation Row - Thread the needle with 2.5m of single thread and tie a keeper bead 15cm from the end. Thread on 4A and 1B. Repeat five times to give you six repeats. Drape the beads around the neck of the bauble - if the beads do not meet together try with 3A or 5A between each of the 6B beads until you get a snug fit (fig 1). Pass the needle through the ring of beads a second time to emerge after the first B bead of the ring.

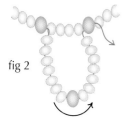

fig 1

**2** The Netted Swags - Thread on 7A, 1B and 7A. Pass the needle through the next B bead of the foundation row to make a loop (fig 2). Repeat five more times to complete the first row of swags. Before you begin the second row of swags you must reposition the needle. Pass the needle down through the first 7A and 1B beads of the first loop to emerge at the far side of the B bead (fig 3). The swags of the second row hang from these B beads at the centre of the first row of swags.

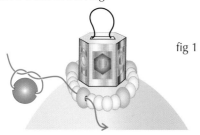

fig 2

fig 3

### Extra Info.....
It can be difficult to hold the bauble safely and bead at the same time. Try out what we do - find a tumbler with a heavy base the same size as the bauble itself. Scrunch up some soft tissue in the tumbler so the bauble can nestle gently but securely leaving you with two free hands to do the beading.

**3** Thread on 8A, 1B, 1A, 1B, 1A, 1B and 8A. Pass the needle through the middle B bead of the next first row loop along (fig 4). Repeat to the end of the row.

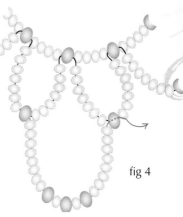

fig 4

The needle must be repositioned for the start of the next row. Pass the needle down through the first 8A, 1B, 1A, 1B, 1A and 1B of the first loop of the row just completed to emerge after the last 1B of the loop. This is the correct position to start the new row.

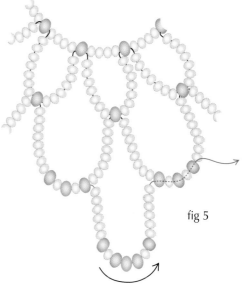

fig 5

**4** Thread on 6A, 1B, 1A, 3B, 1A, 1B and 6A. Pass the needle through the first B bead of the next swag along. Pass the needle through the following four beads of the swag to emerge from the third B bead of the swag (fig 5). Repeat four times.

You will need to complete the row with one more swag. Thread on 6A, 1B, 1A, 3B, 1A, 1B and 6A. Pass the needle through the first 1B, 1A and 1B of the next swag around the bauble (fig 6).The next row hangs from this middle B bead of the second row swag.

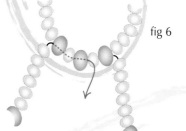

fig 6

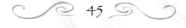

**5** Thread on 11A, 1B, 1A, 1B, 1C, 1A, 1B and 1A. Turn the needle and leaving aside the last three beads threaded to anchor the strand pass the needle back up through the C bead and the B bead above it in the same direction as previously threaded to bring the B bead to sit across the top of the C bead (fig 7).

Thread on 1A, 1B and 11A. Pass the needle through the middle B bead of the next second row swag along (fig 8).

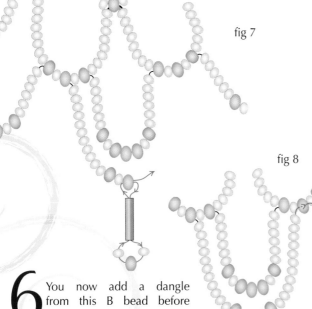

fig 7

fig 8

**6** You now add a dangle from this B bead before making the next swag. Thread on 2A, 1C, 1A, 1B, 1D, 1B and 3A. Turn the needle and leaving aside the last 3A threaded to anchor the strand pass back up the B bead below the D bead and the following 1D, 1B, 1A, 1C and 2A beads to emerge alongside the B bead on the swag. Pass the needle through the B bead at the centre of the swag in the same direction as before (fig 9).

Repeat steps 5 and 6 five more times to complete the row.

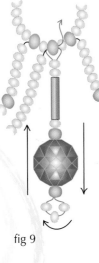

**7** The needle now needs to be repositioned before you start the new row. Pass the needle through the next 1A and 1B and down through the 11A, 1B, 1A and 1B of the first swag of the row just completed. The needle will now be just above the C bead. Pass the needle down through the C bead, one of the A beads below it and the B bead right at the bottom of the dangle. This is where the next row will start and it will link all of the six C bead dangles around the bauble.

fig 9

### Extra Info.....
If you make a mistake remove the needle and pull the thread back through the beads. Do not try to thread the needle back through the beading or you will split the thread and get in a tangle.

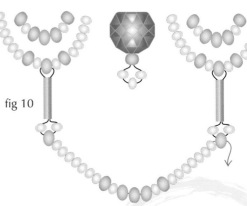

fig 10

fig 11

**8** The Layered Swags & Tails - Thread on 7A, 1B, 1A, 3B, 1A, 1B and 7A. Pass the needle through the B bead at the bottom of the next C bead dangle around the bauble (fig 10).

Thread on 1B. Pass the needle through the B bead at the bottom of the C bead dangle again to draw the new B bead up parallel to the B bead just passed through (fig 11).

Repeat five more times to complete the row around the bauble.

**9** The next row hangs from the single B beads added on the row just completed. Pass the needle through the single B bead just added at the end of the previous row (fig 12). You will notice that the needle is now pointing in the opposite direction.

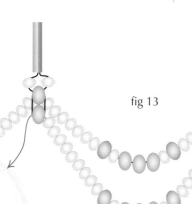

fig 12

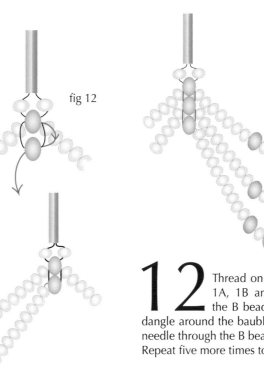

fig 13

fig 16

**10** Thread on 9A, 1B, 1A, 3B, 1A, 1B and 9A. Pass the needle through the single B bead at the bottom of the next C bead dangle around the bauble (fig 13) - note that fig 13 shows the needle travelling in the opposite direction around the bauble. Thread on 1B and pass the needle through the B bead supporting the new swag (fig 14).

Repeat five more times to work right around the bauble.

fig 14

**12** Thread on 10A, 1B, 1A, 1B, 1A, 1B, 1A, 1B, 1A, 1B and 10A. Pass the needle through the B bead at the bottom of the next C bead dangle around the bauble (fig 16). Thread on 1B. Pass the needle through the B bead supporting the new swag (fig 17). Repeat five more times to work right around the bauble.

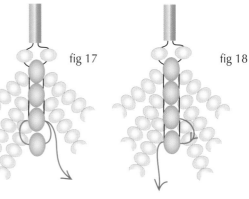

fig 17

fig 18

To reposition the needle for the next row pass the needle through the single B bead just added to the bottom of the last C bead dangle (fig 18) - note that the needle has changed direction again.

fig 15

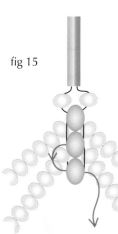

**11** The next row hangs from the single B beads added on the row just completed. Pass the needle through the last single B bead just added (fig 15) - note that the needle has changed direction again.

fig 22

# 15

Thread on 14A, 1B, 1A, 1B, 1A, 1B, 1A, 1B, 1A, 1B and 14A. Pass the needle through the B bead at the bottom of the next C bead dangle around the bauble (fig 22).

# 16

Thread on 4A, 1C, 2A, 1B, 1D, 1B and 3A. Leaving aside the last 3A beads threaded to anchor the strand pass the needle back up the last B bead threaded and the following 1D, 1B, 2A, 1C and 4A to emerge alongside the B bead supporting the new dangle. Pass the needle through this B bead in the same direction as before to centralise the dangle (fig 23).

Repeat steps 15 and 16 five more times to complete the swag pattern for the bauble. Finish off all the thread ends securely.

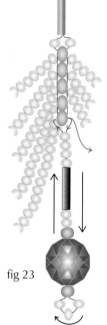

fig 23

# 17

The Hanging Loop - Prepare the needle with 1m of doubled thread and tie on a keeper bead 15cm from the end. Thread on 1A, 1D, 1A, 1B, 1A, 1E, 1B and 1A. Pass the needle through the hanging loop at the top of the bauble. Pass the needle back up the beads just added to emerge alongside the keeper bead (fig 24).

fig 24

# 18

Thread on 1B followed by sufficient A beads to make a loop to hang the bauble from (approximately 40A). Pass the needle back down through the single B bead to draw up the loop and emerge alongside the keeper bead. Remove the keeper bead and tie these thread ends to the needle end of the thread to secure the beading. Pass the needle through a few beads before trimming to neaten. Return to the other thread ends just above the D bead and attach the needle. Pass the needle through a few beads to neaten and trim as before.

# 13

Thread on 12A, 1B, 1A, 1B, 1A, 1B, 1A, 1B, 1A, 1B and 12A. Pass the needle through the B bead at the bottom of the next C bead dangle around the bauble (fig 19). Thread on 1B. Pass the needle through the B bead supporting the new swag (fig 20).

Repeat five more times to work right around the bauble.

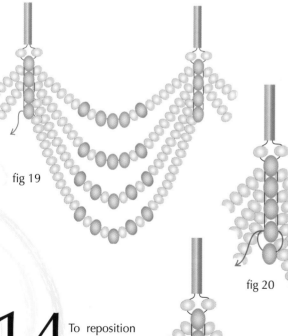

fig 19

fig 20

# 14

To reposition the needle for the last row pass the needle through the B bead just added to the bottom of the last C bead dangle (fig 21) - note that the needle has changed direction again.

fig 21

## Mini Swags & Tails Bauble

This is a reduced version of the Swags & Tails design on a 40mm bauble.

The bead count for step 2 is reduced to 6A, 1B and 6A. The second row adds the bugle bead support for the swags and a 4mm fire polished facet dangle (instead of using a 6mm facet in row three). The swags are shorter and fewer in number but the overall effect is very similar to the 60mm version - just a lot faster to make.

## Theatre Necklace

A simple adaptation of the swags creates a stunning necklace.

Start with the top row - decide on the finished length you need; how many swags you want and which beads to use. This particular design uses 7g of size 10/0 silver lined purple seed beads, 4g of size 8/0 silver lined topaz AB seed beads, thirteen 4mm garnet AB fire polished facets for the dangles and two 6mm facets for the bead tag clasp.

Thread up the top row adding a bead tag and loop to either end (see figs 29 and 30 on page 56) and the correct number of size 8/0 seed beads to support the swags.

Pass the needle back along the top row adding in the extra size 8/0 seed beads that will support the first row of swags (as fig 11 on page 46).

When you have added the last support bead for the first row of swags you can turn the needle and come back along the design to add the swags and the support beads for the next row of swags. Continue until the design is complete.

The swags on this necklace are quite small so they do not need heavier beads along the length to keep them smooth and weighted into place. If you make longer swags think about adding a few extra size 8/0 seed beads to the centres of the swags or enhance the design further with 4mm faceted glass or tiny drop-shaped beads.

# Starry Night Bauble

## You Will Need

### Materials

One 60mm frosted black glass bauble
6g of size 8/0 black seed beads A
10g of size 10/0 silver lined crystal seed beads B
6g of size 3 black twisted bugle beads C
Eleven 6mm black fire polished glass beads D
One 12mm black fire polished bead E
A reel of black size D beading thread

### Tools

A size 10 beading needle
A pair of scissors to trim the threads

A classic design for Christmas or simply to twinkle in the window as it catches the first sunrays of the day. Silver stars on a black or dark blue bauble look spectacular and are reminiscent of the northern sky in the winter but gold stars on purple makes you think of the souk and the smell of incense. The two styles of beaded stars used here give you endless possibilities for more decorative motifs and wearable jewellery.

This Decoration is Made in Four Stages

The first stage makes the large bugle star ring that fits around the widest part of the bauble and supports a fringe of five smaller stars.
The second stage makes a foundation row around the neck of the bauble.
The third stage connects the foundation row to the large star ring and also adds five smaller stars to complete the fringe.
The final stage makes the hanging loop at the top.

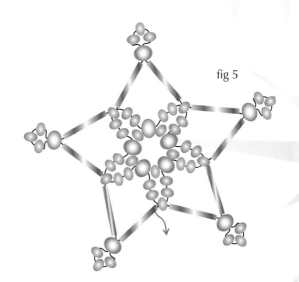

fig 5

1  The Large Bugle Star Ring - Prepare the needle with 1.5m of single thread and tie a keeper bead 15cm from the end.

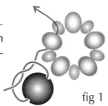

fig 1

2  Thread on 1A, 1B, 1A, 1B, 1A, 1B, 1A, 1B, 1A and 1B. Pass the needle through the first A bead threaded to bring the beads into a ring (fig 1). Thread on 5B. Pass the needle through the next A bead around the ring (fig 2). Repeat around the ring to make five loops of 5B beads. Reposition the needle by passing through the first 3B beads of the first loop of 5B (fig 3).

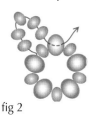

fig 2

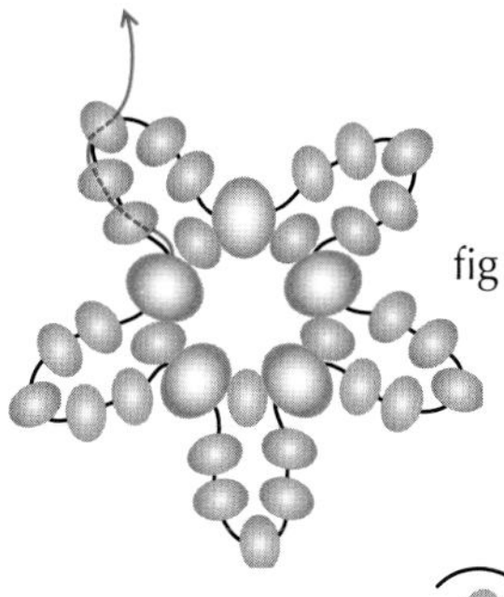

fig 3

3  Thread on 1C, 1A and 3B. Leaving aside the last 3B beads threaded to anchor the strand, pass the needle back through the A bead and add 1C.

Pass the needle through the middle (third) B bead of the next loop around (fig 4).

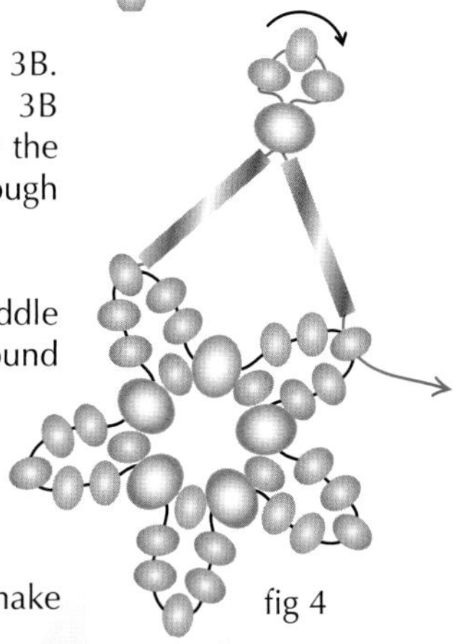

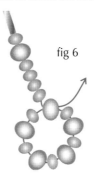

fig 4

Repeat step 3 four more times to make five points in total.

On completion of the large star the needle will emerge through a B bead between two bugle points (fig 5).

4  To make a fringe star, thread on 14B, 1C, 1B, 1A, 4B, 1A, 1B, 1A, 1B, 1A, 1B, 1A, 1B, 1A and 1B. Pass the needle through the fifth to last A bead threaded to form a ring of ten beads (fig 6). Thread on 4B. Leaving aside the last B bead threaded to anchor the strand pass the needle back through the third B bead just added and thread on 2B. Pass the needle through the next A bead around the ring of ten beads (fig 7) to complete the first point on the star.

Repeat to make the second point.

fig 6

fig 7

5  Thread on 3B, 1A, 1D, 1A and 3B. Turn the needle and leaving aside the last 3B beads threaded to anchor the strand, pass it back up through the 1A, 1D, 1A and 3B to make a spike of beads (fig 8). Pass the needle through the A bead on the ring in the same direction as before to centre the spike below the star and make the third and fourth points of the star as before.

fig 8

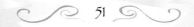

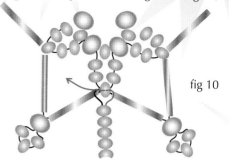

**7** Pass the needle through the following 1A, 1B, 1C and 14B beads to emerge at the bottom edge of the large bugle star. Pass the needle through the B bead of the bugle star in the same direction as before to bring the fringe strand to dangle centrally below the bugle star (fig 10).

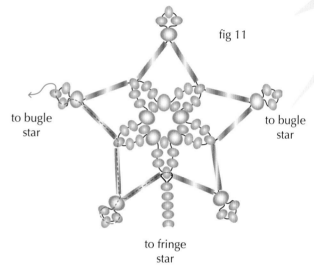

fig 10

The needle now needs to be repositioned for the next bugle star. Referring to fig 11 pass the needle through the middle B bead at the very tip of the second star point (fig 11).

fig 11

to bugle star

to bugle star

to fringe star

**8** Before you start the next star you must add a bridging bead. Thread on 1A. Pass the needle through the B bead at the end of the star point in the same direction as before and back through the A bead (fig 12) to bring the two beads parallel to one another. Thread on 1B. Pass the needle through the A bead just added and the new B bead to bring this new bead parallel to the other two (fig 13) - this last B bead will become the tip of the next star.

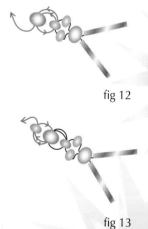

fig 12

fig 13

**6** Thread on 2B. Locate the 4B beads that link this star to the strand below the bugle star. Pass the needle up through the 2B beads before the A bead that sits below the bugle to complete the star (fig 9).

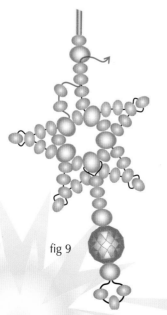

fig 9

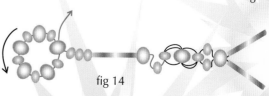

fig 14

**9** Thread on 1B, 1A, 1C, 3B, 1A, 1B, 1A, 1B, 1A, 1B, 1A, 1B, 1A and 1B. Pass the needle through the fifth to last A bead to draw the last ten beads up into a ring (fig 14).

**10** Thread on 5B. Pass the needle through the next A bead around the ring. Repeat three more times to complete four loops of 5B around the ring.

For the fifth loop thread on 2B and pass the needle through the B bead directly below the C bead (fig 15). You are now in the correct position to make the bugle points as before.

fig 15

Thread on 1C, 1A and 3B. Leaving aside the last 3B beads threaded to anchor the strand pass the needle back through the A bead. Thread on 1C and pass the needle through the middle B bead of the next loop of 5B around the ring (as in fig 4). Repeat to complete four points in total.

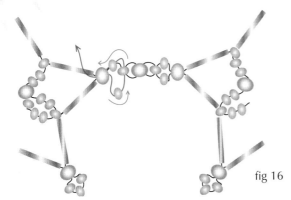

fig 16

**11** To start the fifth point thread on 1C. Pass the needle through the A bead above the first C bead of this star. Add 1B bead and pass the needle through the end B bead of the bridge from the last star. Pass the needle through the following 1B and 1A back towards the star just made (fig 16) to complete the second bugle star.

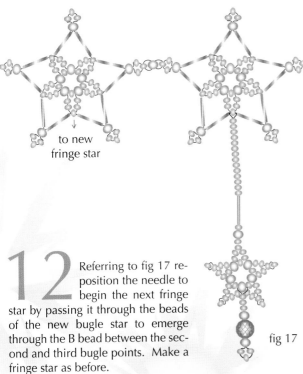

to new fringe star

fig 17

**12** Referring to fig 17 reposition the needle to begin the next fringe star by passing it through the beads of the new bugle star to emerge through the B bead between the second and third bugle points. Make a fringe star as before.

**13** After completing the fringe star bring the needle up through the beads of the bugle star to reposition the needle for the next motif. Add a bridging bead as in fig 12; make a further bugle star and add another fringe star below it.

Repeat to complete a row of five bugle stars with five fringe stars. Finish with the needle emerging through the correct bead on the last bugle star as if about to start a sixth star. The band of linked stars now needs to be brought together into the ring that will sit around the bauble.

fig 18

**14** Thread on 1A and link onto the last B bead of the last star as in fig 12. Pass the needle through the end B bead on the point of the first star (as located in fig 11) and back through the A bead (fig 18). Repeat the stitch to make the join secure and finish off the thread end securely.

The completed ring of stars should now fit snugly over the bauble (and slip straight off again!)

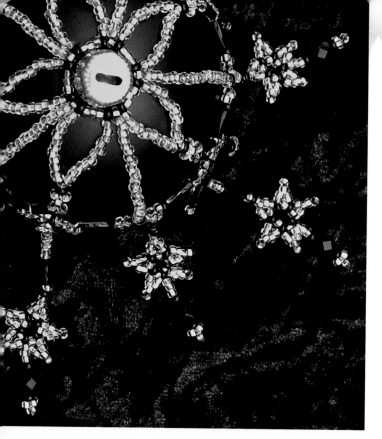

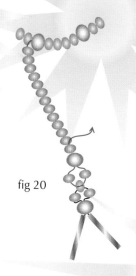

## 16
Making the Connection - Slip the ring of large bugle stars over the bauble and try to hold in place around the centre of the bauble.

Return to the foundation row and thread on 13B, 1A and 1B. Pass the needle through the middle B bead at the top of the top bugle spike of the closest bugle star. Thread on 1B and pass the needle back up through the A bead and the following 1B bead (fig 20). Thread on 12B. Pass the needle through the A bead on the foundation row immediately before the A bead where you started, to bring the needle through to point towards the start of the loop just created (fig 21).

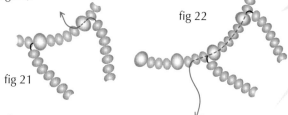

fig 20

fig 22

fig 21

## 17
Referring to fig 22 pass the needle through the following beads of the ring to emerge from the middle B bead of the next section around the suspension ring. (If your next section has an even number of B beads bring the needle out through the gap between the centre two B beads).

## 18
Thread on 22B. Pass the needle down through the bridging A bead between the bugle star just linked onto and the next bugle star around (fig 23). You are now in the correct position to make the fringe strand and star. Refer back to the instructions in steps 4, 5 and 6 to work the strand and star. Bring the needle back up through the beads of the strand, through the bridging A bead and the 22B above it to the edge of the suspension ring.

## 15
The Foundation Row - This sits around the neck of the bauble and connects to the top points of the bugle stars. In-between the bugle stars it drops down five further fringe strands.

First you need to make a relatively tight band of beads around the neck of the bauble. Due to manufacturing differences the neck size of baubles will vary from supplier to supplier - the bead sequence given below is the ideal, however it may not suit your particular bauble. The important part of the pattern is that you end up with 10A beads spaced evenly around the neck of the bauble - add or subtract B beads as necessary to get a good fit.

Prepare the needle as in step 1 and thread on 1A, 4B, 1A and 3B. Repeat four more times (45 beads in total). Pass the needle through the first 1A, 4B and 1A beads to bring the beads into a ring (fig 19).

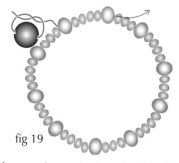

fig 19

This loop should fit snugly over the neck of the bauble (if you need to adjust the B bead count try to do so in all of the alternate sections to keep the spacing even).

fig 23

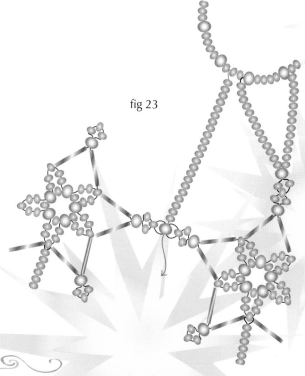

### Extra Info....
Most of the designs in this book use two sizes of seed beads and one bugle bead. These designs match the larger seed bead and the bugle to the colour of the bauble. In this bauble design the bugle beads make up a large part of the pattern so you may wish to use a contrast colour bugle for the large stars e.g. try gold bugles on a red bauble.

**19** Pass the needle through the B bead on the ring where the needle emerged in the same direction as before to centre the strand below the bead (see fig 24) (if you had an even number of beads in the gap pass the needle through the central gap once more) and through the next B bead around the ring. Pass the needle through the following beads of the ring to emerge at the far side of the second A bead around (fig 24) ready to start the next connection to the top of the next bugle star around the girdle.

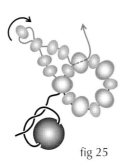

fig 24

new fringe
star

bugle star

**20** Repeat the beading in steps 16, 17, 18 and 19 to add the remaining links to the tops of the bugle stars and the last four fringe strands and stars. Finish off the thread end securely.

**21** The Hanging Loop - Prepare the needle as in step 1. Thread on 1A and 1B. Repeat four more times (10 beads). Pass the needle through the first A bead to make a ring. Thread on 4B. Leaving aside the last A bead threaded to anchor the strand pass the needle back through the third B bead of the 4B just added. Thread on 2B and pass the needle through the next A bead around the ring (fig 25). Make four more points in a similar fashion.

fig 25

**22** Bring the needle through the first four beads of the first point made to emerge at the tip of the point. Thread on 1A, 1B, 1D, 1B, 1A and 50B. Pass the needle back down through the last A bead threaded to draw the 50B up into a loop (fig 26).

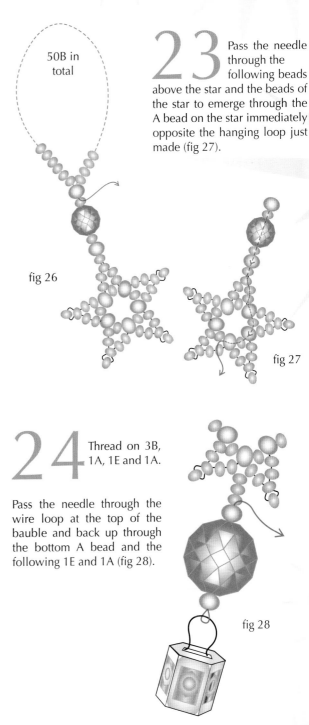

50B in
total

**23** Pass the needle through the following beads above the star and the beads of the star to emerge through the A bead on the star immediately opposite the hanging loop just made (fig 27).

fig 26

fig 27

**24** Thread on 3B, 1A, 1E and 1A.

Pass the needle through the wire loop at the top of the bauble and back up through the bottom A bead and the following 1E and 1A (fig 28).

fig 28

**25** Run the needle back up to the edge of the star, through the A bead on the edge of the ring at the centre of the star to centralise the strand, then around the B and A beads of the ring. Bring the needle back down through the beads above the wire loop, through the loop once more and back up to the ring of A and B beads to reinforce the connection.

Now pass the needle back up through the beads of the star so you can also reinforce the 50B beads of the hanging loop.

Finish off the thread ends securely.

# Starry Night Inspirations

The star motifs used on the Starry Night Bauble can be made in quantity to produce garlands and delicate hanging strands for the tree but they can also be the start of more versatile projects. Simple earring drops, pendants, fancy necklaces and tassels can all be built up around the stars. The ideas on these pages work alongside the Starry Night instructions - the bead references A, B, C refer back to the sizes and shapes of the original recipe for the bauble although the colours have changed as you can see.

## Starstruck Necklace

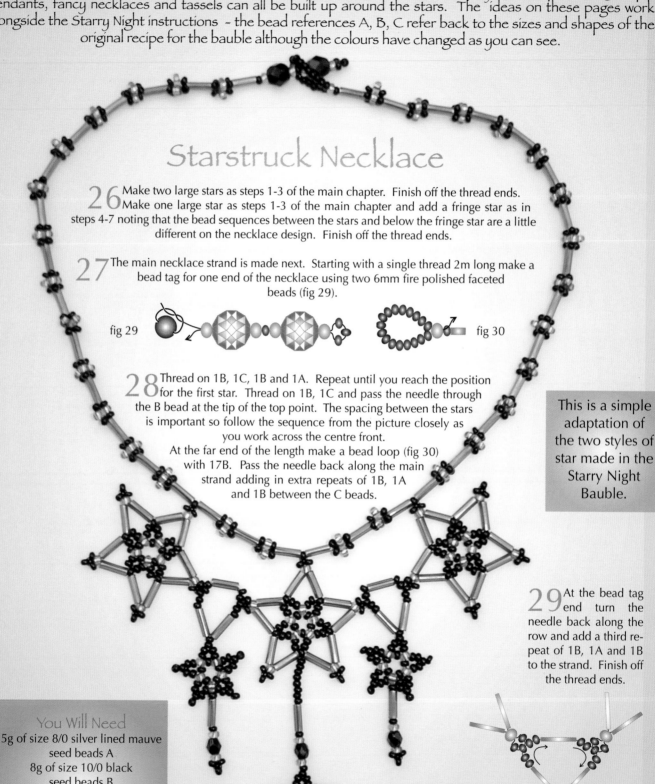

26 Make two large stars as steps 1-3 of the main chapter. Finish off the thread ends.
Make one large star as steps 1-3 of the main chapter and add a fringe star as in steps 4-7 noting that the bead sequences between the stars and below the fringe star are a little different on the necklace design. Finish off the thread ends.

27 The main necklace strand is made next. Starting with a single thread 2m long make a bead tag for one end of the necklace using two 6mm fire polished faceted beads (fig 29).

fig 29          fig 30

28 Thread on 1B, 1C, 1B and 1A. Repeat until you reach the position for the first star. Thread on 1B, 1C and pass the needle through the B bead at the tip of the top point. The spacing between the stars is important so follow the sequence from the picture closely as you work across the centre front.
At the far end of the length make a bead loop (fig 30) with 17B. Pass the needle back along the main strand adding in extra repeats of 1B, 1A and 1B between the C beads.

This is a simple adaptation of the two styles of star made in the Starry Night Bauble.

29 At the bead tag end turn the needle back along the row and add a third repeat of 1B, 1A and 1B to the strand. Finish off the thread ends.

fig 31

## You Will Need
5g of size 8/0 silver lined mauve seed beads A
8g of size 10/0 black seed beads B
6g of size 3 transparent purple AB bugle beads C
Three 6mm black fire polished faceted beads D
Four 4mm black fire polished faceted beads E

30 For the small star links; start a new thread and following fig 31 make a link between the first and central large stars. With reference to the photograph add a fringe star with a small dangle below. Finish off the thread ends and repeat on the other side of the design.

# Eight Pointed Star

1 Thread on 1A and 2B and repeat eight times. Pass the needle through the beads a second time to make a ring. Bring the needle through to emerge through an A bead.

2 Thread on 2B, 1C, 1B, 1A and 1B. Pass the needle back down the A bead to pull the last B bead up tightly to the A bead. Thread on 1B, 1C and 2B. Pass the needle through the next A bead around the ring (fig 32).

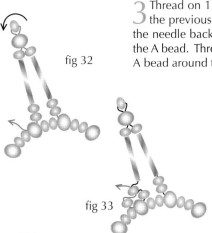

fig 32

fig 33

3 Thread on 1B. Pass the needle up through the B bead adjacent to the previous C bead (fig 33). Thread on 1C, 1B, 1A and 1B. Pass the needle back down the A bead to pull the last B bead up tightly to the A bead. Thread on 1B, 1C and 2B. Pass the needle through the next A bead around the ring.

Repeat step 3 right around the ring - make sure that you link the last point of the star to the first point through the B bead adjacent to the first bugle.

4 You will need to make the star a little stiffer to hold the shape firmly. Pass the needle through the beads of the central ring twice and the points of the star once. If the needle will pass through the holes in the beads of the ring again, repeat. Finish off the thread ends securely.

## Sunburst Tassel

Make an eight pointed star with size 10/0 silver lined crystal seed beads, size 8/0 silver lined gold seed beads and size 3 silver lined gold bugles. At the tip of one point stitch a 4mm jump ring in place to carry the tassel.

On the opposite point of the star thread on the beads for the suspension loop - this design uses an 8mm crystal AB fire polished faceted bead to accent the loop.

Referring to the tassel techniques in the Net and Tassel Bauble chapter (page 29) make a tassel starting with a 4mm jump ring and 6mm crystal AB fire polished facet for the top bead. Make three different length tassel strands with a 12 x 8mm crystal AB fire polished faceted drop at the bottom of each strand.

Link the two jump rings together to complete the design.

## Midnight Pendant

Make an eight pointed star with size 10/0 black seed beads, size 8/0 silver lined red seed beads and size 3 silver lined red bugles. Extend three of the points with a few extra seed beads and some 12 x 8mm fire polished faceted drops to form the dangles.

Extend the opposite point of the star out with a few extra seed beads and a 6mm fire polished facet. Use one size 10/0 seed bead right at the top to take the necklace strand.

String the necklace strand from matching beads. If you want to add a bead and loop clasp see the instructions for the Starstruck Necklace opposite.

This design also makes a stunning pair of earrings - just stitch a 4mm jump ring to the top of the star and attach the earfitting.

# Emperor Bauble

## You Will Need

### Materials

One 60mm frosted purple glass bauble
3g of size 10/0 silver lined teal seed beads A
5g of size 8/0 silver lined bronze seed beads B
10g of size 10/0 transparent teal AB seed beads C
10g of size 10/0 frosted purple seed beads D
4g of size 6/0 transparent purple AB seed beads E
2g of size 6/0 frosted silver lined blue AB seed beads F
Sixteen 6mm scarab blue fire polished faceted beads G
One 12mm purple fire polished bead H
A reel of purple size D beading thread

### Tools

A size 10 beading needle
A pair of scissors to trim the threads

Mughal Badshah Shah Jahan, the creator of the Taj Mahal, sat on the Peacock Throne at his palace in Delhi. Fit for the Emperor of such a powerful domain, the gold and enamelled throne was set with fantastic jewels including the Koh-i-Noor diamond, huge rubies, emeralds and pearls. It was carried off to Persia as a trophy of war and later destroyed in transit during a storm at sea. It remains only in poetry and legend as a thing of incalculable value and fabled beauty.

## This Decoration is Made in Five Stages

First you will make the fringed peacock feather motifs.
The unfringed motifs with dangling strands are second.
Then the foundation row around the neck of the bauble is made.
The motifs are strung together next and attached to the foundation row.
The hanging loop is added to complete the design.

**1** The Fringed Motif - Prepare the needle with 1.5m of single thread and tie a keeper bead 15cm from the end. Thread on 1G, 1F and 10A. Pass the needle through the 1G and 1F beads to bring the 10A beads into a strap (fig 1). Thread on 10A. Pass the needle through the 1G and 1F beads again to make a second strap of 10A to the other side of the G and F beads (fig 2).

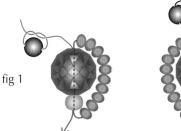

fig 1       fig 2

**2** Thread on 4A. Leaving aside the last 3A beads to anchor the strand pass the needle back through the first of the A beads just added and the following 1F and 1G (fig 3). Pass the needle through the 10A beads to one side of the 1G and 1F beads; through the 3A beads of the anchor and the 10A beads to the other side of the 1G and 1F beads. Pass the needle through the following 12A beads to emerge through the middle A bead of the anchor (fig 4).
Pull the thread quite firmly so all of the A beads sit snugly against one another.

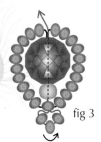  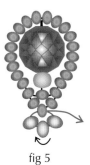

fig 3      fig 4

fig 5

**3** Thread on 3B. Pass the needle through the middle bead of the 3A anchor to draw the beads into a tight loop (fig 5).

Pass the needle through the 3B beads just added, the middle A bead of the anchor and the 3B beads once more to make the work a little more firm (fig 6).

fig 6

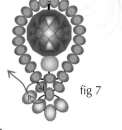 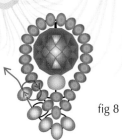

fig 7       fig 8

**4** Thread on 1B. Pass the needle through the adjacent A bead of the 3A anchor towards the middle A bead of the anchor. Pass the needle through the new B bead in the same direction as before to bring the two beads parallel to one another (fig 7). This is square stitch - you will notice that the thread follows a square path through the beads.

Thread on 1B. Square stitch this new 1B bead to the second A bead along this side of the motif (fig 8).

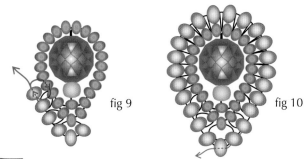

fig 9       fig 10

**5** Thread on 1B. Square stitch this new 1B to the next A bead along this side of the motif (fig 9).

Repeat step 5 sixteen times to bring you 2A beads away from the 3B beads added in fig 5.

**6** Thread on 1B and square stitch to the second of the 2A beads (the A bead adjacent to the middle A bead of the anchor). Pass the needle through the first 2B beads added to emerge through the B bead at the tip of the motif (fig 10).

Pass the needle through all of the B beads just added to re-emerge through the B bead at the bottom of the motif as fig 10.

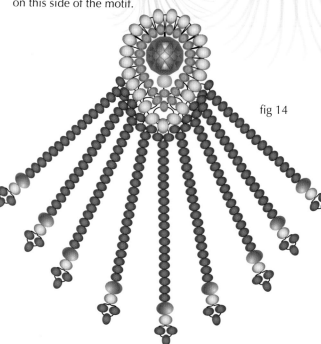

**9** Repeat step 8 from this new needle position using 19C to start the strand and passing back up just 18C before adding the extra 1C and passing through the B bead at the top of the strand. Pass through the following B bead around the motif.

Repeat the same technique from this B bead starting with 18C to make the next strand. Now repeat with 17C from the next 1B along the edge to complete the shortest fringe strand on this side of the motif.

fig 14

**7** Thread on 21C, 1E, 1B and 3C. Leaving aside the last 3C beads threaded pass the needle back up through the 1B, 1E and the following 20C only.

Thread on 1C and pass the needle through the B bead at the tip of the motif in the same direction as before (fig 11).

Pass the needle through the following 1B bead of the motif (fig 12).

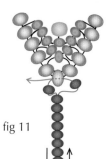

fig 11

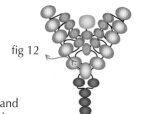

fig 12

**8** Thread on 20C, 1E, 1B and 3C. Leaving aside the last 3C beads threaded pass the needle back up through the 1B, 1E and the following 19C only.

Thread on 1C and pass the needle through the B bead at the top of the strand in the same direction as before (fig 13).

Pass the needle through the following 1B bead of the motif.

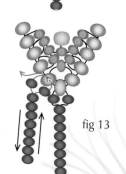

fig 13

**10** Pass the needle through the following B beads to emerge on the opposite edge of the motif through the fourth B bead from the first fringe strand. Beginning with a count of 17C make a mirror image set of fringe strands from these four B beads (fig 14).

Finish off the thread end without blocking the holes in the B beads around the top edge of the motif. Remove the keeper bead and finish off this end similarly.

Make a further four identical motifs and set aside for now.

**11** The Unfringed Motif & Hanging Strand - Following steps 1 to 6 make the central section of the feather motif.

Finish with the needle emerging through the B bead at the tip of the motif (as fig 10).

**12** Thread on 45D, 2B, 1D, 1A, 1G, 1F and 10A. Pass the needle through the 1G and 1F beads to bring the 10A beads into a strap around the side of the 1G and 1F (fig 15) - note the needle does not pass through the A bead immediately above the G bead.

45D in total

fig 15

# 13

As before thread on 10A and pass the needle through the 1G and 1F beads to make the second strap. Thread on 4A. Leaving aside the last 3A beads to form the anchor pass back up the 1A, 1F, 1G and the bottom 1A bead of the main strand (fig 16).

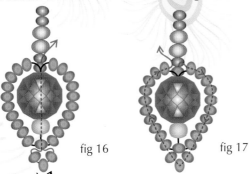

fig 16                                        fig 17

# 14

Pass the needle through the 10A beads down the first side of the new motif; the 3A of the anchor and the 10A up the second side of the motif (fig 17) to bring the beads into line. Pass the needle up through the bottom 1D and 1B of the strand (fig 18).

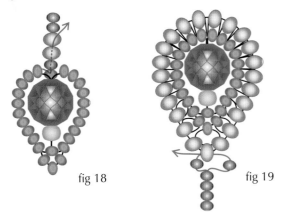

fig 18                                        fig 19

# 15

Pass the needle through the following 1B and 44D to emerge 1D below the first motif. Thread on 1D and pass the needle through the B bead at the tip of the first motif in the same direction as before (fig 19).

Finish off the thread end securely without blocking any of the holes in the B beads on the edge of the motif. Remove the keeper bead and finish this end similarly.

Repeat steps 11 - 15 four more times to make five identical motifs.

# 16

The Foundation Row - Prepare the needle with 1.5m of single thread and tie a keeper bead 15cm from the end. Thread on five repeats of 1E and 5D. Pass the needle through the first 1E bead in the same direction as before to draw the beads into a circle.

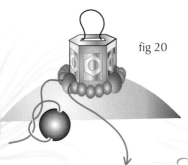

fig 20

# 17

Drop the circle over the neck of the bauble (fig 20). The ring needs to fit snugly without the thread showing between the beads.

If you need to adjust the D bead count between the E beads do so now - you need five equally spaced E beads around the neck of the bauble. When you have made any necessary adjustments, check the fit and pass the needle through the beads of the ring once more to firm up the shape and remove from the bauble. It is easier to make the next stage without the bauble in situ.

Ensure that the needle is emerging from an E bead.

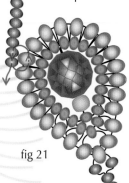

# 18

Stringing Up - Thread on 12D. Pick up the first un-fringed motif. Starting with the middle B bead at the tip of the motif as number one, count up the side of the motif until you reach B bead number ten.

Pass the needle through this tenth B bead with the needle pointing away from the tip of the motif.

Pass the needle through the last 2D beads threaded in the same direction as originally threaded so that the 1B bead and 2D beads sit parallel to one another (fig 21). This is another example of square stitch.

fig 21

# 21

Thread on 2D and square stitch to the next 1B bead along the top edge of the fringed motif.

Repeat the last stitch four more times (fig 24) (6B beads in total). Pass the needle through the beads of the last stitch worked again to make sure that the work is firm.

fig 24

# 19

Pass the needle through the beads of the last stitch once more to make sure that the connection is firm.

Thread on 2D. Square stitch these 2D to the next 1B bead down the edge of the motif (fig 22).

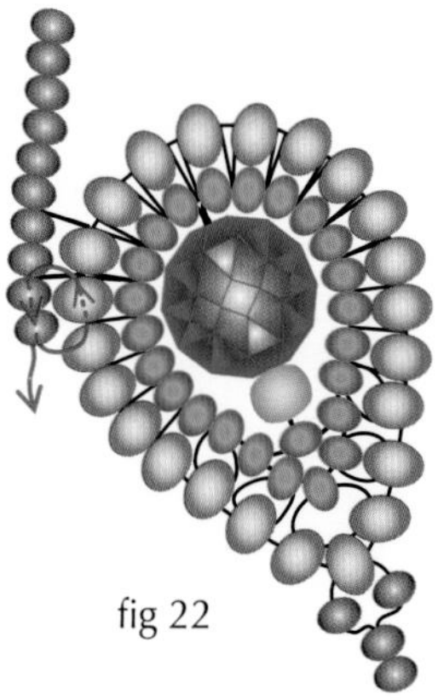

Thread on 2D and repeat the stitch to the next 1B down the edge.

Make two more similar stitches adding 2D beads to each of the next 2B beads down the edge of the motif (5B beads in total).

Pass the needle through the beads of the last stitch once more to make sure the work is firm.

fig 22

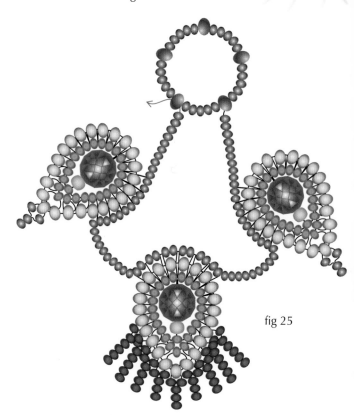

fig 25

# 20

Thread on 12D. Pick up the first of the fringed motifs and locate the fifth B bead up from the last fringe strand.

fig 23

Pass the needle through this fifth B bead with the needle pointing towards the fringes on this side of the motif. Pass the needle through the last 2D beads threaded in the same direction as before (fig 23). This is square stitch again. Pass the needle through the beads of the stitch once more to make sure that the work is firm.

# 22

Referring to fig 25 thread on 12D. Pick up the second unfringed motif. Starting with the middle B bead at the tip of the motif as number one count up the side of the shape until you reach B bead number six.

Pass the needle through this sixth B bead with the needle pointing towards the tip of the motif. Pass the needle through the last 2D beads threaded in the same direction as before to complete the square stitch. Pass the needle through the beads of this stitch once more to make sure the work is firm. Thread on 2D and square stitch to the next 1B bead up the edge of the motif.

Repeat the last stitch three more times (5B beads in total). Pass the needle through the beads of the last stitch once more to make firm.

# 23

Thread on 10D and pass the needle through the next E bead around the foundation row (fig 25) - take special note of which side the thread passes through the E bead - the loop just created in steps 18-22 hangs between the D beads of the ring only.

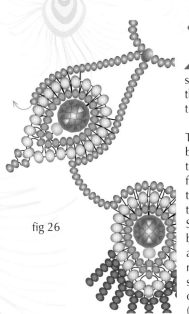

fig 26

# 24
You now need to repeat the stringing sequence to add the remaining seven motifs to the design.

Thread on 12D. Referring back to step 18 count up the other side of the unfringed motif just added to the design to locate the tenth B bead from the tip. Square stitch this tenth B bead to the last 2D beads added to start the repeat making four more square stitches to attach this side of the motif onto the string (fig 26).

# 25
Referring to fig 27 you can see how the motifs all slot into the design. The fringed pendants attach across the 6B beads along the top edge of the motif whilst the unfringed pendants attach through 5B beads to either side of the motifs.

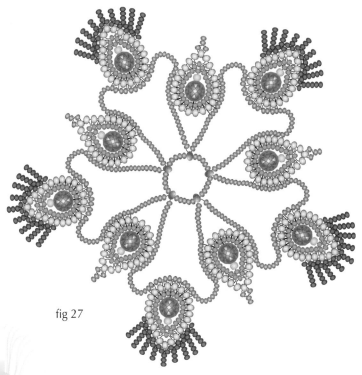

fig 27

Work around the foundation row adding in the motifs as you see in fig 27. Remember to double stitch the first and last square stitches of each sequence to make the work firm.

When all ten motifs are attached pass the needle through all of the D beads added since step 18 to smooth out the beading and make it a little stronger. If the needle will fit through the holes of the D beads once more repeat the pass. Finish off all of the thread ends securely and place the completed net over the bauble.

# 26
The Hanging Loop - Prepare the needle with 1.5m of single thread and tie a keeper bead 15cm from the end. Following steps 1 to 6 make the central section of the feather motif.

# 27
Pass the needle through the B beads at the edge of the motif to emerge through the thirteenth B bead from the tip of the shape (counting the bead at the tip as number one).

Thread on 2A, 1B, 1H, 1B and 1F. Pass the needle through the loop at the top of the bauble and back up the 1F, 1B, 1H and 1B beads just added. Thread on 2A. Pass the needle through the twelfth and thirteenth B bead at the edge of the motif to centre the strand just created (fig 28).

Pass the needle through the new sequence two more times to make sure the connection is strong.

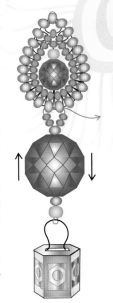

fig 28

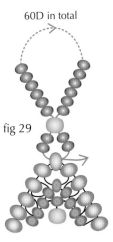

60D in total

fig 29

# 28
Pass the needle through the B beads of the motif to emerge through the B bead at the tip of the shape.

Thread on 2D, 1F and 60D. Pass the needle back down the F bead to draw up the loop and thread on 2D. Pass the needle through the B bead at the tip of the motif in the same direction as before (fig 29). Pass the needle through the beads of the new sequence twice more to make sure the loop is strong before finishing off the thread ends.

# Anatolia Bauble

## You Will Need

### Materials

One 60mm frosted purple glass bauble
10g of size 10/0 silver lined gold seed beads A
8g of size 3 purple bugle beads B
8g of size 8/0 silver lined purple seed beads C
Twenty-two purple 4mm fire polished faceted beads D
Four purple 6mm fire polished faceted beads E
One purple 12mm fire polished faceted bead F
A reel of size D purple beading thread

### Tools

A size 10 beading needle
A pair of scissors to trim the threads

This heavily beaded design is inspired by the close-fitting beaded headdresses of traditional Middle Eastern dancers and the fantasy costumes of the Tales of Sinbad which the big movie studios turned into sumptuous productions in the 1930's and 40's. Filigree cartouches adorned the hairlines falling onto the forehead with swags of jewels stretching around the sides of the head framing the face with stranded tassels and twinkling fringes.

## The Decoration is Made in Several Stages

A ladder-stitched ribbon that bends around to form three interlinked drop-shaped loops.

These loops are then decorated with swags and tassel strands.

A suspension ring around the neck of the bauble links the decorated loops to the bauble.

A hanging loop is added to complete the design.

**1** The Ladder-Stitched Ribbon - Prepare the needle with 2m of thread and tie a keeper bead 15cm from the end. Thread on 1B, 1A, 1C, 1A, 1B, 1A, 1C and 1A. Pass the needle back up through the first B bead threaded and the following 1A, 1C, 1A and 1B to bring the beads into a long rectangular shape (fig 1) - this is the basic ladder stitch technique.

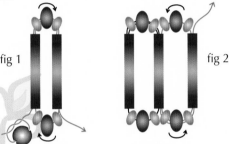

fig 1          fig 2

**2** Thread on 1A, 1C, 1A, 1B, 1A, 1C and 1A and pass the needle down the last B bead of the previous stitch to bring the new bugle parallel to the previous bugle. Pass the needle through the following 1A, 1C, 1A and 1B of the new stitch to complete this rung of the ladder (fig 2).

You now need to start to shape the ladder into a curve. The shaping is achieved by reducing the small bead count between the bugle beads on one edge of the ladder.

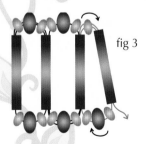

fig 3

fig 4

**3** Thread on 1A, 1B, 1A, 1C and 1A. Pass the needle through the B bead of the previous stitch and back through the single A bead and the B bead of the new stitch (fig 3). Thread on 1A, 1C, 1A, 1B and 1A. Pass the needle through the B bead of the previous stitch and the following 1A, 1C, 1A and 1B of the new stitch (fig 4). You will see that by leaving just 1A between the bugles of the ladder on one edge that the ladder has started to curve. You will also notice that the threading bead sequence alternates - the next stitch will start with a single A bead before the B bead and the following stitch will begin with 1A, 1C and 1A.

fig 5

**4** Referring to fig 5 work 15 more rungs of the ladder using 1A on the inside of the curve and 1A, 1C and 1A on the outside. Finish off with two rungs using 1A, 1C and 1A on both the inside and the outside of the curve (fig 5) (22 B beads in total).

fig 6

**5** Thread on 1A, 1B, 1A, 1B and 1A. Pass the needle through the B bead on the other end of the ribbon bringing the needle through to emerge at the inside edge of the curve. Thread on 1A and pass the needle through the last bugle of the ladder to bring the ends of the ladder together on the inside of the curve forming a diamond shape at the top of the loop. Pass the needle through the following 1A, 1B, 1A and 1B just added (fig 6).

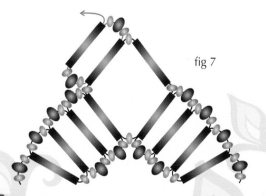

fig 7

**6** Thread on 1A, 1C, 1A, 1B, 1A, 1C and 1A. Pass the needle through the B bead on the side of the diamond shape just completed to bring the new B bead parallel to it. Pass the needle through the following 1A, 1C, 1A and 1B just added (fig 7).

7 Referring to fig 8 thread on 1A, 1C, 1A, 1B, 1A, 1C and 1A and repeat as the previous stitch to add another rung to the ladder. The new ladder needs to be shaped slightly so thread on 1A, 1C, 1A, 1B and 1A. Make the stitch as before. The next stitch is 1A, 1C, 1A, 1B, 1A, 1C and 1A but the following one needs to be 1A, 1C, 1A, 1B and 1A to shape the ladder once more (see fig 8). Complete this ladder with two stitches of 1A, 1C, 1A, 1B, 1A, 1C and 1A (fig 8).

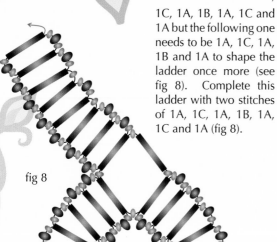

fig 8

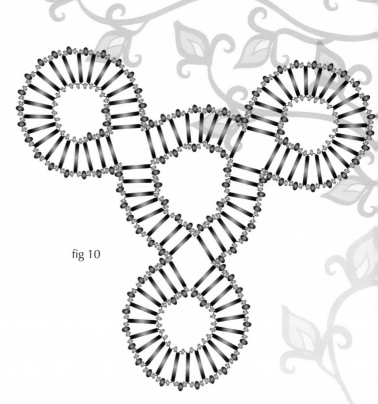

fig 10

8 Thread on 1A, 1B, 1A, 1B, 1A, 1B and 1A. Pass the needle through the last B bead of the ladder to bring the new beads up into a diamond shape at the end of the ladder. Pass the needle through the following 1A, 1B, 1A and 1B of the new diamond to be in the correct position to start the new loop of ladder stitch (fig 9).

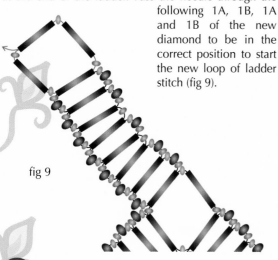

fig 9

9 Start the next loop with two stitches of 1A, 1C, 1A, 1B, 1A, 1C and 1A. Referring to fig 10 you can see that you now need to start shaping the loop as before. The first shaping stitch will be 1A, 1B, 1A, 1C and 1A. Look at fig 10 - this loop needs to come around in an anticlockwise direction - make sure your work is curving the right way. Work as with the previous loop to complete sixteen more shaping stitches bringing the end of the ladder around towards the diamond made in fig 9. Make one stitch with 1A, 1C, 1A, 1B, 1A, 1C and 1A. The next stitch needs to link up with the edge of the diamond.

10 Thread on 1A, 1C and 1A. Pass the needle through the B bead on the edge of the diamond to bring the last B bead added parallel to it. Thread on 1A, 1C and 1A and pass the needle through the B bead of the previous stitch to close up the link. Pass the needle through the first 1A, 1C and 1A bead of this stitch and through the B bead of the diamond once more to complete the stitch. You have now completed two loops and one link.

11 Reposition the needle through the beads of the diamond to emerge through the B bead on the blank side of the diamond (opposite the present needle position). Work the link to the next loop as in fig 8 - be careful of the shaping as the two single A beads need to fall on the inside edge of the link - refer to fig 10.

12 Having completed the link as in fig 8 you will need to make a diamond of 1A, 1B, 1A, 1B, 1A, 1B and 1A to support the third loop, as in fig 9.

Referring to fig 10 make the third loop as for the second loop. Make sure that you connect it up to the correct sides of the diamond and you shape the correct edge of the ladder so that it curves smoothly into place.

To complete the arrangement as in fig 10 make a third link as in fig 8 to the vacant side of the first diamond - make sure that you shape the link on the inside edge only and remember that the last B bead on the link as seen on fig 8 is already in situ as the side of the diamond you are joining onto (see fig 10).

13 Referring to fig 11 pass the needle through the beads of the adjacent diamond to emerge through the A bead at the base of the diamond and closest to the top of the first loop. Thread on 1A, 1E and 1A. Pass the needle through the A bead on the opposite side of the diamond. Turn the needle and pass it back down the second A bead just added; the E bead and the first A bead to bring them into a straight line down the centre of the diamond. Pass the needle through the A bead at the base of the diamond in the same direction as before. Pass the needle through the first 1A, 1C, 1A bead combination on the inside edge of the loop and thread on 1A. Pass the needle through the next 1A, 1C, 1A bead combination on the inside of the loop pulling the new A bead into the gap at the end of the B bead.

Thread on 1A and pass through the next A bead on the inside edge of the loop.

fig 11

**14** Repeat right around the inside edge of the loop adding 1A between all the A beads of the shaped section and 1A between the 1A, 1C, 1A bead combination at the end of the sequence. Complete the sequence by passing through the A bead at the base of the diamond.

Work the needle through the beads of the link to the next diamond and loop around and repeat steps 13 and 14. Repeat for the last diamond and loop.

**15** Adding beads to the inner edge of the loops has drawn the loops up a little more firmly than before. The outer edge of the loops now needs to be reinforced. Bring the needle through the adjacent B bead and the following 1A down the outside edge of the loop. Pass the needle through the following 1C, 2A, 1C, 2A around the edge of the loop. Repeat until you reach the other end of this edge of the loop. Pull the thread quite firmly and you will see the gap between the A beads close up and the loop will become much firmer. Do not pull too hard or the loop will pucker and deform.

**16** Pass the needle through the next A bead at the corner of the diamond and along through the A and C beads of this outer edge of the ribbon between this loop and the next. Pull the thread through to close up the gaps between the A beads along this edge. Pass the needle through the A bead at the corner of the next diamond and on around the outer edge of the next loop. Repeat until you have taken the needle right around all of the outer edge of the shape as seen in fig 10. Pass the needle through an adjacent B bead to emerge on the inside edge of the ribbon triangle which supports the three loops. Run the needle through the A and C beads of this inner edge to reinforce.

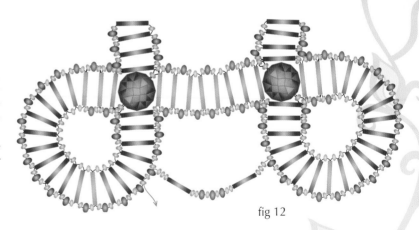

fig 12

**17** The Swags And Tassels - If necessary join on a new thread and bring the needle down through the outer edge beads of one of the loops to emerge through the seventh A bead (just above the fourth C bead) along. Thread on 3A, 1B, 2A, 1C, 1A, 1C, 1A, 1C, 2A, 1B and 3A. Taking the needle across to the outer edge of the adjacent loop, pass the needle down through the fourth C and eighth and ninth A beads of the outer edge of the next loop to emerge just before the fifth C bead (fig 12). Pull the needle through so that the beads of the swag touch one another and the beads of the loop edges (do not worry if this seems a little tight as the swags will fall into curves when in place over the round shape of the bauble).

fig 13

**20** Referring to fig 16 start the next strand with 5A, 1B, 1A, 1B, 1A, 1C, 1A, 1B, 2A, 1C, 1A, 1D, 1A, 1C and 3A. Leaving aside the last 3A threaded to anchor the strand pass the needle back up through the last C bead threaded and the following beads to emerge just before the first A bead of the sequence. Thread on 1A and pass the needle through the ninth C bead of the loop and the following three beads to emerge at the far side of the tenth C bead.

**18** Thread on 5A, 1B, 2A, 1C, 1A, 1C, 1A, 1C, 2A, 1B and 5A. Taking the needle back across to the outer edge of the first loop, pass through the fifth C bead and the following tenth and eleventh A beads to emerge just before the sixth C bead (fig 13). The last swag is 7A, 1B, 2A, 1C, 1A, 1C, 1A, 1C, 2A, 1B and 7A. Take the needle across to the adjacent loop and pass through the sixth C bead of that edge and the following six beads to emerge from the eighth C bead of the outer edge (fig 14).

**21** Thread on 2A, 1C, 1A, 1B, 1A, 1B, 1A, 1B, 1A, 1C, 1A, 1B, 2A, 1C, 1A, 1D, 1A, 1C and 3A. As before turn the needle and leaving the last 3A beads to anchor the strand pass back up the remaining beads to emerge just before the first A bead of the strand. Thread on 1A and pass the needle through the tenth C bead and the following three beads to emerge at the far side of the eleventh C bead (the central C bead). Thread on 9A, 1C, 1A 1B, 1A, 1B, 1A, 1B, 1A, 1C, 1A, 1B, 2A, 1C, 1A,1D, 1A, 1C and 3A. Complete the strand as before adding the single A bead at the top of the strand and passing through to emerge through the next C bead around the loop edge.

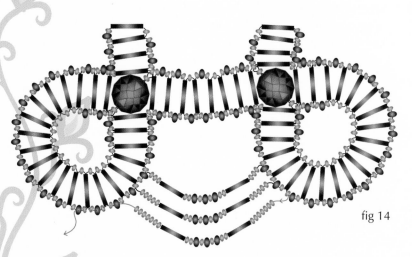

fig 14

**19** Thread on 5A, 1B, 1A, 1C, 1A, 1B, 2A, 1C, 1A, 1D, 1A, 1C and 3A. Leaving aside the last 3A threaded to anchor the strand pass the needle back up through the last C bead threaded and the following fifteen beads to emerge just before the first A bead of the sequence.

Thread on 1A and pass the needle through the eighth C bead of the outer edge of the loop in the same direction as before and the following three beads to emerge from the ninth C bead of the edge (fig 15). A tassel strand will hang from this C bead and the next five C beads of the edge.

fig 15

fig 16

**22** Make three tassel strands to this side of the loop to match those on the other side of the longest tassel strand (fig 16).

Having completed the seven tassel strands pass the needle up through the A and C beads at the edge of the loop to emerge through the fourth C bead from the top of the loop. This is the correct place to begin a matching set of swags between this edge of the loop and the next loop around. Follow steps 17 and 18 (figs 12 - 14) to add a set of swags. Continue to work around the loops to add another set of tassels; a final set of swags and a final set of tassel strands so that the beading matches up all around the interlinked loops.

# 23
The Suspension Ring - Prepare the needle with 1m of single thread and tie a keeper bead 15cm from the end. Before you make the ring you will need to check the bead count required to make the correct fit around the neck of your bauble - to test out your bauble thread on 30A. Drape the 30A around the neck of the bauble - it needs to sit just underneath the bottom of the metal cap - does it fit well? If it is too tight add 3A or 6A; if it is too loose remove 3A or 6A. Make a note of the correct number of beads and remove them from the thread. Make sure the keeper bead is in place and thread on one third of the bead count just noted.

fig 17

# 26
The Hanging Loop - Prepare the needle with 1m of single thread and tie a keeper bead 15cm from the end. Thread on 1A, 1C, 1A and 1F. Pass the needle through the metal hanging loop at the top of the bauble and back up the 1F, 1A, 1C and 1A beads. Thread on 1A, 1B, 1A, 1B, 1A, 1B, 1A and 1B (fig 19).

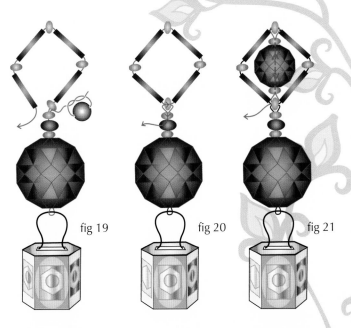

fig 19    fig 20    fig 21

# 27
Pass the needle through the first A bead of the sequence in the same direction as before to draw the B beads into a diamond shape. Pass the needle down through the first A bead towards the top of the bauble (fig 20). To reinforce the thread loop through the metal hanger pass the needle down through the 1C, 1A and 1F beads, through the loop and back up through the same beads to emerge through the A bead at the bottom of the diamond. Thread on 1A, 1E and 1A. Pass the needle through the A bead at the top of the diamond and back down through the three beads just added. Pass the needle through the A bead at the bottom of the diamond in the same direction as before (fig 21).

fig 18

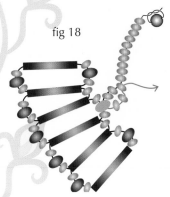

# 24
Thread on 3A. Pick up the interlocking loops and pass the needle through the C bead in the middle of the inner edge of the link between two of the loops (fig 17 shown in pink highlight). Thread on 2A. Pass the needle up through the first of the 3A beads just added (fig 18).

# 25
Thread on the next third of the bead count noted earlier. Thread on 3A and pass the needle through the next highlighted bead (see fig 17) around the inner edge of the links between the loops. Thread on 2A and as fig 18 pass up through the first of the 3A just added. Thread on the last third of the bead count. Thread on 3A and pass the needle through the last highlighted bead around the inner edge of the links between the loops. Thread on 2A and as fig 18 pass up through the first of the 3A just added. Remove the keeper bead and tie this end of the thread securely to the needle end pulling the knots down between the beads to conceal. Pass the needle through a few beads to neaten the end and trim. Reattach the needle to the other end of the thread and neaten similarly before trimming.

Slip the completed suspension ring over the top of the bauble so that the loops fall into place around the circumference of the bauble.

# 28
Pass the needle back up through the three beads in the centre of the diamond and the A bead at the top of the diamond and thread on 1C, 1A, 1D, 1A and 1C followed by 60A beads to make a hanging loop. Pass the needle back down the 1C, 1A, 1D, 1A and 1C beads to draw up the loop (fig 22). You may wish to reinforce the hanging loop further by passing the needle through the A bead at the top of the diamond and back up and around the hanging loop. Finish off the thread end securely.

Remove the keeper bead and attach the needle to this end of the thread. Finish off this end of the thread and neaten similarly.

fig 22

# Snowstorm Bauble

## You Will Need

### Materials

One 60mm frosted white glass bauble
10g of size 10/0 silver lined crystal seed beads A
4g of size 10/0 frosted crystal seed beads B
4g of size 3 silver lined crystal bugle beads C
2g of size 8/0 silver lined crystal seed beads D
Nineteen 4mm crystal fire polished faceted beads E
One 6mm crystal fire polished faceted bead F
A reel of white size D beading thread

### Tools

A size 10 beading needle
A pair of scissors to trim the threads

On a crisp December night you can stare up into the blackness of the sky and see the first few snowflakes of winter spiralling down towards you. This design is very dramatic when made over a dark-coloured bauble or scintilatingly sparkly when made over a sugary-toned paler ornament. This design is decorated with six-pointed large and small snowflake motifs - the motifs need to be made with a constant tension in the thread to make sure that the arms stick out at equidistant angles.

### This Decoration is Made in Three Stages

The foundation row around the neck of the bauble.
The hanging snowflakes. in two sizes, that drape over the bauble shape.
The hanging loop.

**1** The Foundation Row - Prepare the needle with 1.5m of single thread and tie a keeper bead 15cm from the end. Thread on 6B, 1D, 6B, 1D, 6B, 1D, 6B and 1D. Drape the beads around the neck of the bauble to make a ring.

**2** Check the fit of the beads around the bauble neck - it needs to be quite tight with no thread showing between the beads. If necessary alter the B bead count between the D beads - you need to have 4D beads equally spaced around the circumference of the bauble neck. When you are happy with the fit pass the needle through the beads one more time to bring them into a circle (fig 1).

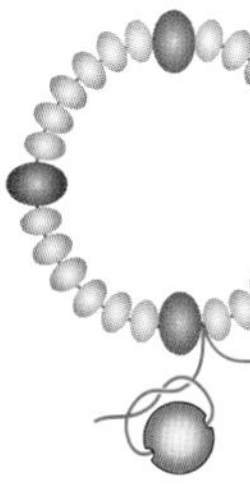

fig 1

**3** Remove the keeper bead and tie the two ends of the thread together securely with a double knot. Pass the needle through the beads of the ring to emerge through the next D bead around. Take the ring off the top of the bauble and work without the bauble in the way. Thread on 15B to start the first of the large snowflakes.

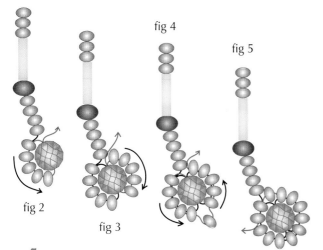

fig 2

fig 3

fig 4

fig 5

**4** The Large Snowflake - Thread on 3A, 1C, 1D, 9A and 1E. Pass the needle through the last 5A of the 9A just threaded and the following E bead (fig 2) to draw the 5A beads into a strap around the side of the E bead. Thread on 5A. Pass the needle through the E bead once more to draw the new beads into a strap to the other side of the E bead (fig 3). Pass the needle through the first 5A beads around the E bead. Thread on 1A. Pass the needle through the following 5A strap around the E bead (fig 4) to draw the new bead into the gap above the hole in the E bead. Thread on 1A and pass the needle through the first 2A of the first strap (fig 5).

**5** Thread on 4A, 1D, 1C and 3A. Turn the needle and leaving aside the last A bead threaded to anchor the strand pass the needle back through the 2A beads immediately adjacent to make a tiny stick of beads (fig 6).

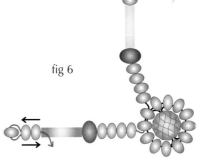

fig 6

Thread on 3A. As before leave aside the last A bead as an anchor and pass the needle back through the previous 2A and the following 1C and 1D beads (fig 7). Adjust the tension in the thread so that the two short sticks of beads sit in a V shape at the end of the C bead. Thread on 3A.

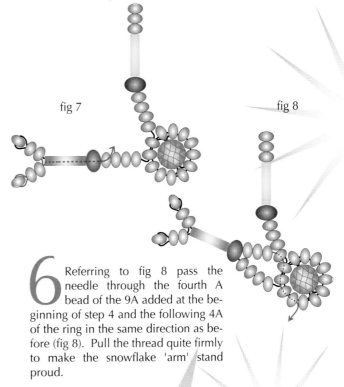

fig 7

fig 8

**6** Referring to fig 8 pass the needle through the fourth A bead of the 9A added at the beginning of step 4 and the following 4A of the ring in the same direction as before (fig 8). Pull the thread quite firmly to make the snowflake 'arm' stand proud.

## Extra Info.....

Normally when you choose a thread colour to work your beading you select a colour that tones with the majority of the bead shades. When you are beading over an object like a bauble you need to take that colour into account as well. Here the white thread will disappear against the white glass of the bauble.

**7** Repeat step 5. This new 'arm' needs to link back to the ring through the first A bead threaded in the previous arm.

Referring to fig 9 pass the needle through the first A bead of the previous arm and the following 4A beads of the ring.

**8** Thread on 4A, 1D, 1C and 3A. This arm now extends down into a tassel which carries a smaller snowflake motif*.

Thread on 11B.

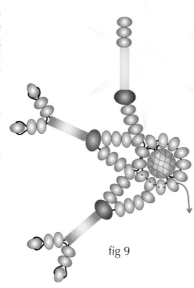

fig 9

**9** The Small Snowflake - Thread on 1A, 1C, 6A and 1E. Pass the needle through the last 5A of the 6A just added and the following E bead (fig 10). Thread on 5A and pass the needle through the E bead again to make the second strap (as fig 3). Referring to fig 4 pass the needle through the first 5A beads around the E bead. Thread on 1A. Pass the needle through the following 5A strap around the E bead (as fig 4) to draw the new bead into the gap above the hole in the E bead. Thread on 1A and pass the needle through the first <u>4A</u> of the following strap (fig 11).

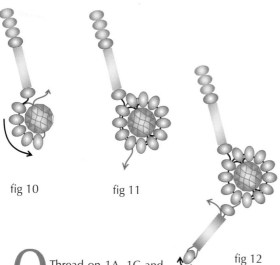

fig 10          fig 11

fig 12

**10** Thread on 1A, 1C and 1A. Turn the needle and leaving aside the last A bead threaded to anchor the strand pass the needle back through the C bead (fig 12). Thread on 1A. Pass the needle through the 2A beads of the ring immediately before the start of this spike and the following 2A (fig 13). Adjust the tension in the thread so that the 2A beads at the base of the C bead sit side by side and hold the spike firmly in place.

fig 13

**11** Repeat step 10 four more times. The needle should now be emerging through the second A bead on the ring past the start of the motif (fig 14). Thread on 1A and pass the needle up through the first C bead and the following A bead at the top of the motif (fig 15). Tension the thread to make the six spikes of the motif all stand out at the correct angles.

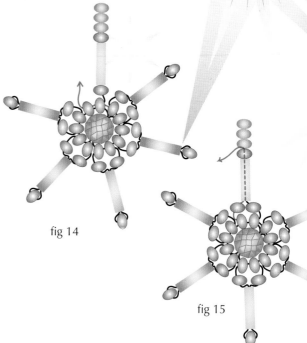

fig 14

fig 15

fig 16

**12** Pass the needle up through the B beads above the small snowflake to emerge 3B beads below the large snowflake.

Thread on 3B and 3A.

Pass the needle up through the C bead and the following 1D on the incomplete arm of the large snowflake (fig 16).

Thread on 3A.

You can now complete this arm of the snowflake by passing the needle through the first A bead of the previous arm and the following 4A beads of the ring (fig 17).

Work one more large snowflake arm as before.

For the next arm work as before but on the final stage pass the needle through the first 2A beads on the ring only to emerge at the start of the arm just made (fig 18).

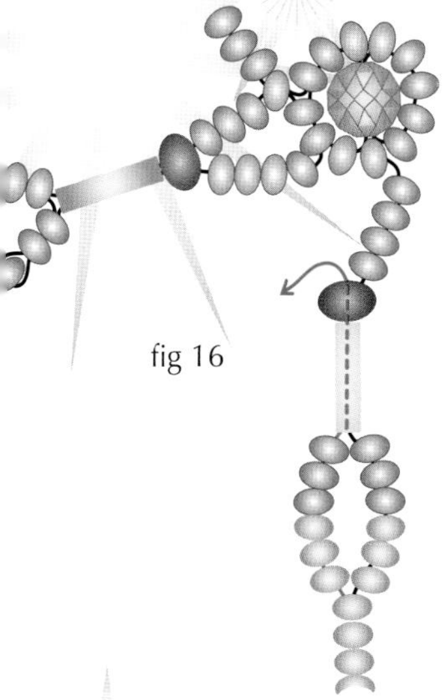

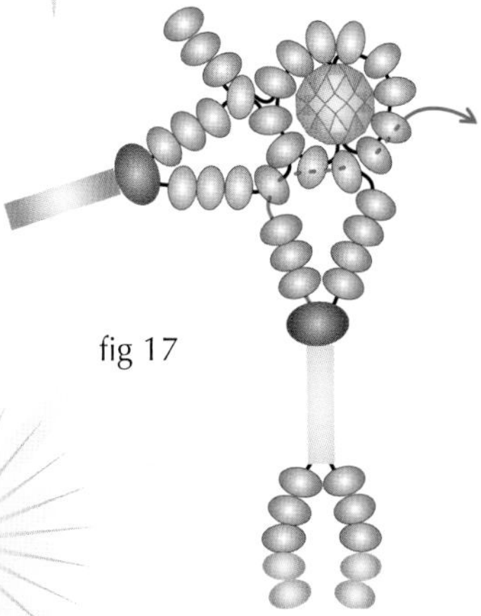

fig 17

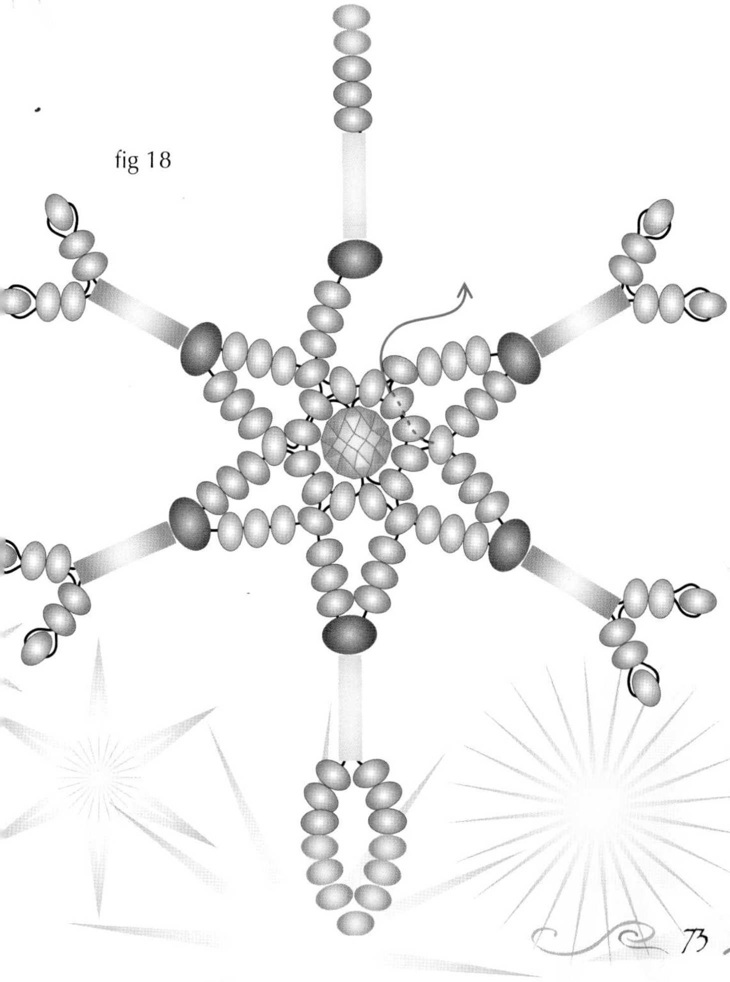

fig 18

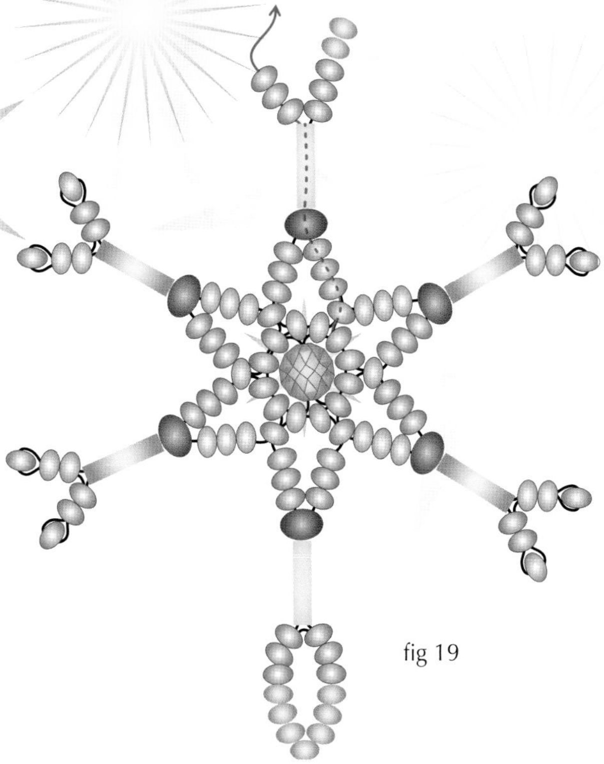

fig 19

**13** Pass the needle up through the first A bead of the arm just completed and thread on 3A. Pass the needle up through the 1D and 1C of the beads that you added at the beginning of the large snowflake and thread on 3A (fig 19). Tension the thread so that the snowflake lies flat with the arms all at the correct angles. Thread on 15B. Pass the needle through the next D bead around the ring made in step 2 (fig 20).

fig 20

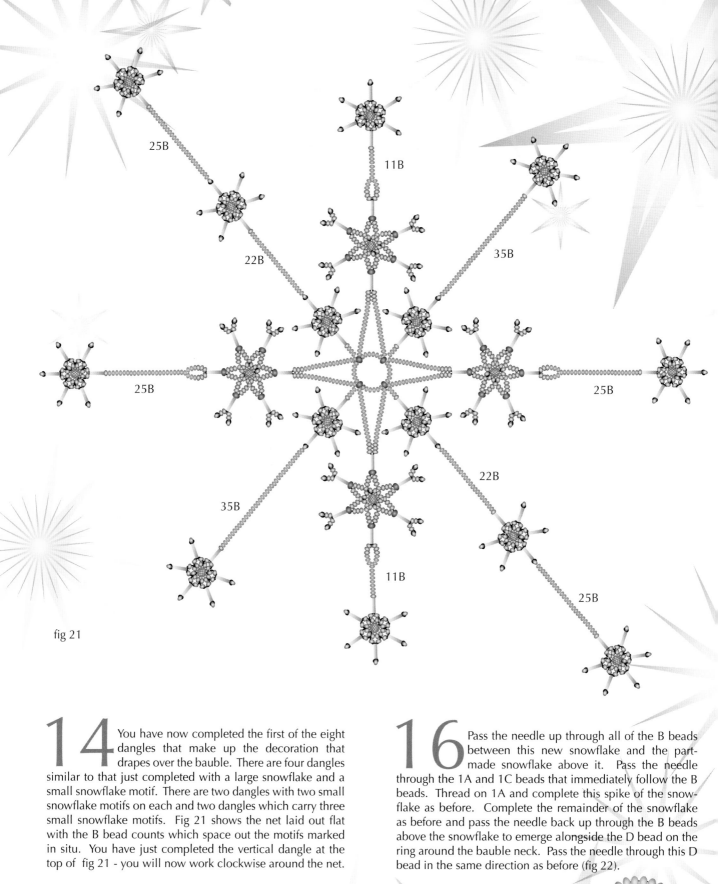

25B

11B

22B

35B

25B

35B

22B

25B

11B

25B

25B

fig 21

**14** You have now completed the first of the eight dangles that make up the decoration that drapes over the bauble. There are four dangles similar to that just completed with a large snowflake and a small snowflake motif. There are two dangles with two small snowflake motifs on each and two dangles which carry three small snowflake motifs. Fig 21 shows the net laid out flat with the B bead counts which space out the motifs marked in situ. You have just completed the vertical dangle at the top of fig 21 - you will now work clockwise around the net.

The next dangle around has two small snowflake motifs.

**15** Thread on 3B. Repeat steps 9 and 10. Repeat step 10 once more to make a second full spike. Thread on 1A, 1C and 1A. This arm now extends down into a tassel strand which will support the second small snowflake on this strand**. Thread on 35B. Repeat steps 9, 10 and 11 to make the small snowflake at the end of the dangle strand.

**16** Pass the needle up through all of the B beads between this new snowflake and the part-made snowflake above it. Pass the needle through the 1A and 1C beads that immediately follow the B beads. Thread on 1A and complete this spike of the snowflake as before. Complete the remainder of the snowflake as before and pass the needle back up through the B beads above the snowflake to emerge alongside the D bead on the ring around the bauble neck. Pass the needle through this D bead in the same direction as before (fig 22).

fig 22

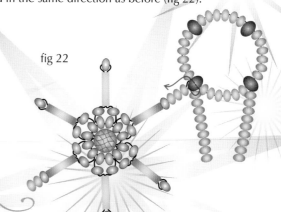

**17** By referring back to fig 21 you can see that the next dangle to make has a large snowflake and a small snowflake to dangle below it. Thread on 15B to start the sequence - now make this dangle as for the first dangle made in steps 4 to 13 inclusive but this time extend the B bead count between the two snowflakes to 25B instead of the 11B used previously.

**18** Referring to fig 21 the next dangle has three small snowflakes in a row. Work step 15 down to **. Now thread on 22B before you start the second snowflake of the dangle. Repeat step 15 down to **. Now thread on 25B before you start the third snowflake of the dangle. Work steps 9, 10 and 11 to complete this third snowflake. Now work the needle back up to the top of the dangle strand working the necessary arms to complete the other two snowflakes. At the top of the dangle pass the needle through the D bead on the ring around the neck of the bauble (see fig 22).

You have now completed half of the dangles. The next four dangles are an exact repeat of the first four dangles. Work the remaining dangles and finish off the thread end securely. Finish off any other thread ends securely before trimming.

Place the completed net over the neck of the bauble.

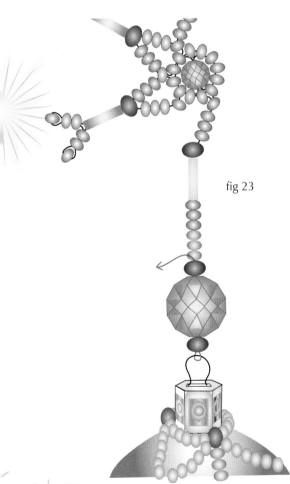

fig 23

**19** The Hanging Loop - Prepare the needle with 1.5m of single thread and tie a keeper bead 15cm from the end. Thread on 4B. Start a large snowflake by working from step 4 to the * in step 8. Thread on 3B, 1D, 1F and 1D. Pass the needle through the wire hanger at the top of the bauble. Pass the needle back up through the 1D, 1F and 1D beads just added to bring the beads up tightly to the top of the wire hanger on the bauble (fig 23).

**20** Thread on 3B and 3A. Pass the needle up through the adjacent 1C and 1D beads of the partly made snowflake arm. Thread on 3A so that you can complete this arm of the snowflake. Work around the snowflake as before to complete the motif finishing with 3A beads which will sit alongside the first 3A beads threaded in step 19.
Thread on 3B and pass the needle up through the very first B bead added in step 19 (fig 24).

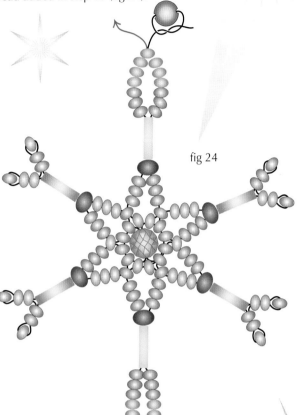

fig 24

**21** Thread on 60B. Pass the needle back down the single B bead which you passed up through in fig 24 to draw the 60B beads up into a loop.

The loop will need to be re-inforced. Take the needle down through the beads of the snowflake to the ring of A beads around the E bead. Pass the needle through these beads so you can turn its direction to once again pass back towards the 60B bead loop. Work the needle back up through the beads of the snowflake to run the thread through the 60B bead loop to make it a little stronger. If you can get the needle through the beads once more it would be prudent to take the needle back down to the thread loop around the wire hanger at the top of the bauble and reinforce that in a similar manner. Finish off all the thread ends securely.

## Extra Info.....
If the snowflakes are a little soft their shape will not hold firmly - you can remedy this with a little clear nail varnish. Working in a well-ventilated area take the decoration off the bauble and lay it flat on a sheet of polythene. Arrange the spikes of the snowflakes correctly. Paint a very thin coat of clear nail varnish onto the beads of the snowflakes and allow to dry thoroughly. The varnish will trickle down between the beads and stiffen the threads. Once the varnish is completely dry, flip the beading over and repeat. You may wish to repeat once more. Do not get the varnish onto the frosted beads between the snowflakes - it will spoil the frosted finish on the beads.

# Byzantium Bauble

✸ ✸ ✸ ✸

## You Will Need

### Materials

One 60mm frosted purple glass bauble
10g of size 10/0 silver lined gold seed beads A
5g of size 8/0 silver lined purple seed beads B
10g of size 3 transparent purple AB bugle beads C
Thirty-six 4mm purple AB fire polished faceted beads D
Sixteeen 6mm purple AB fire polished faceted beads E
Four 8mm purple fire polished faceted beads F
Two 12mm purple fire polished faceted beads G
A reel of purple size D beading thread

### Tools

A size 10 beading needle
A pair of scissors to trim the threads

*B*yzantium conjours images of antiquity, religious iconography and wars between kings. The centre of the Medieval world for commerce, scholarship and cultural interchange Byzantium bridged the gap between Europe and the mysterious lands further east - places of silks, spices, astrology and alchemy.

This Decoration is Made in Five Stages

A cross-shaped grid of seeds, facets and bugles is constructed and draped over the bauble.
The grid is tightened to fit the spherical shape.
The four tassels around the sides of the decoration are added.
The central tassel to the bottom of the bauble is made.
The hanging loop at the top completes the design.

**1** The Grid - Prepare the needle with 2m of single thread and tie a keeper bead 15cm from the end. Thread on four repeats of 1A, 1B, 1A and 1C. Pass the needle through the first 1A bead in the same direction as before to bring the beads into a square shape (fig 1).

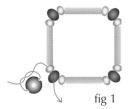
fig 1

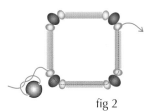
fig 2

**2** Pass the needle through the following 1B, 1A, 1C, 1A, 1B, 1A and 1C (fig 2). Thread on 1A, 1B, 1A, 1C, 1A, 1B, 1A, 1C, 1A, 1B, 1A, 1C, 1A, 1B and 1A. Pass the needle through the last C bead threaded through on the previous square to make a second square alongside the first (fig 3).

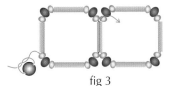
fig 3

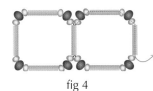
fig 4

**3** Reposition the needle as before by passing through the following 1A, 1B, 1A, 1C, 1A, 1B, 1A and 1C (fig 4).

Thread on 1A, 1B, 1A, 1C, 1A, 1B, 1A, 1C, 1A, 1B, 1A, 1C, 1A, 1B and 1A. Pass the needle through the last C bead threaded through on the previous square to make a third square alongside the second square. Reposition the needle as before to emerge through the C bead at the end of the row (fig 5).

fig 5

Repeat until you have a row of squares eleven units long (see fig 6).

**4** Referring to fig 6 pass the needle back through the beads of the squares to emerge through the C bead of the middle square along the side of the row (fig 6).

**5** Thread on 1A, 1B, 1A, 1C, 1A, 1B, 1A, 1C, 1A, 1B, 1A, 1C, 1A, 1B and 1A. Pass the needle through the C bead along the side of the middle square of the initial row. Reposition the needle as before by passing the needle through the following 1A, 1B, 1A, 1C, 1A, 1B, 1A and 1C of the new square (fig 7).

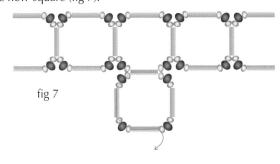
fig 7

**6** Make four more squares in a row out from this new square (fig 8).

Pass the needle through the beads of the new squares (as fig 6) to emerge through the C bead on the opposite edge of the middle square from fig 6.

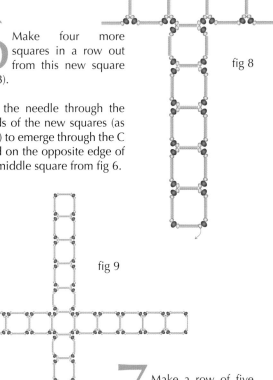
fig 8

fig 9

**7** Make a row of five squares from this side of the first row to complete a cross-shaped grid (fig 9).

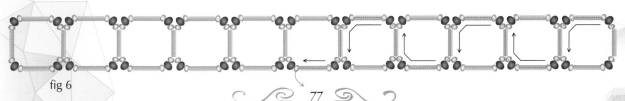
fig 6

**8** As before reposition the needle to emerge through the end C bead of the row. Pass the needle through the following 1A, 1B, 1A, 1C and 1A beads.

Thread on 1D. Referring to fig 10 pass the needle through the A bead immediately preceding the next C bead down this edge of the grid and the following 1C and 1A (fig 10).

fig 10

**9** Thread on 1D. Pass the needle through the A bead preceding the next C bead down the edge and the following 1C and 1A (as fig 10).

Repeat step 9 two more times.

**10** Thread on 1D. Pass the needle through the 1A bead immediately preceding the next 1C along the edge (which in this case is at 90° to the previous C bead) and the following 1C and 1A (fig 11).

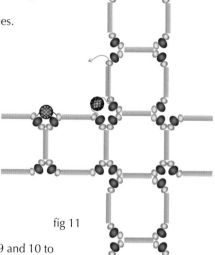

fig 11

Repeat the stitches in steps 9 and 10 to add 1D at the intersections of all of the squares of the grid (36D in total).

Place the centre square of the grid over the neck of the bauble so the four arms of the grid drape down over the sides of the bauble.

fig 12

**11** Tightening the Grid to Fit the Bauble - Pass the needle through the beads of the work to emerge through the end C bead of one of the four arms of the grid. Bring the ends of the arms closely together at the bottom of the bauble.

Thread on 1A, 1B, 1A, 1C, 1A, 1B and 1A. Pass the needle through the C bead at the end of the next grid arm around the bottom of the bauble. Repeat the last stitch until you have linked all four of the arms together (fig 12).

The grid will probably still be quite loose on the bauble shape - you now need to tighten up the beading at the bottom of the bauble.

**12** Bead sizes and bauble sizes vary a little from the manufacturers' stated dimensions so you may need to make an adjustment in the A bead count on the next stitch to make your beading fit your bauble properly.

Pass the needle through the following 1A, 1B and 1A of the last row worked and thread on 3A (you may need to adjust this count from 1A up to 6A). Pass the needle through the last bugle added on the previous row (fig 13) (note the direction of working has changed from the last row).

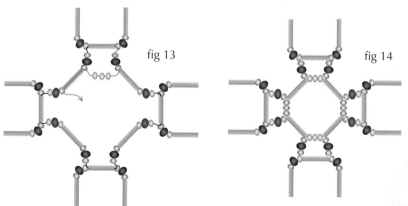

fig 13                fig 14

Repeat the stitch three more times and pull the thread firmly (fig 14). This row should pull the beading in tightly at the bottom of the bauble.

If it is still a little loose and you have reduced the bead count to 1A in step 12 go back to step 11. Unpick the work to the start of step 11 and work this step with just 2A, 1B and 2A on each stitch. On step 12 use 1A and pass through the B bead at the centre of the step 11 stitch to close up the beading at the bottom of the bauble.

If you have less than 50cm of thread remaining finish off the end securely and prepare the needle with a new 1.5m length.

# 13

The Side Tassels - Pass the needle through the beads of the grid to emerge pointing downwards from the second D bead down the edge of one of the grid rows (fig 15).

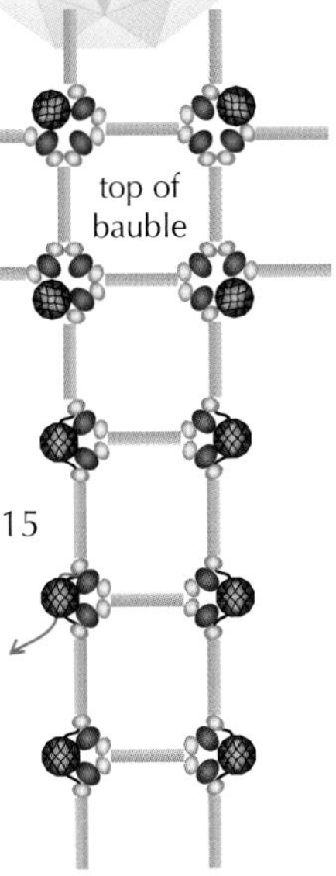

top of bauble

fig 15

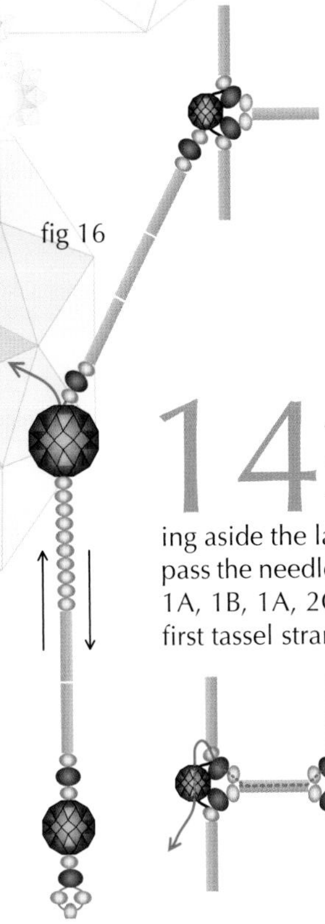

fig 16

# 14

Thread on 1A, 1B, 1A, 3C, 1A, 1B, 1A, 1F, 10A, 2C, 1A, 1B, 1A, 1E, 1A, 1B and 3A. Leaving aside the last 3A beads to anchor the strand pass the needle back up through the 1B, 1A, 1E, 1A, 1B, 1A, 2C, 10A and 1F beads to form the first tassel strand (fig 16).

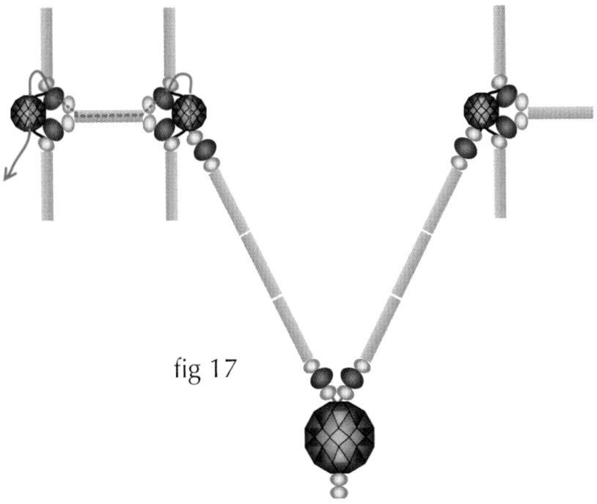

fig 17

# 15

Thread on 1A, 1B, 1A, 3C, 1A, 1B and 1A. Pass the needle up through the second D bead on the closest edge of the next grid arm around the bauble (see fig 17) to stretch the tassel support into a V- shape across the gap between the grid arms.

Pass the needle through the adjacent 1B, 1A and 1C to move the needle across the width of the grid arm. Referring to fig 17 pass the needle up through the following 1A and 1B and down through the 1D bead on the far edge of the grid arm ready to begin the next tassel support (fig 17).

Repeat steps 14 and 15 three more times to add a tassel support and the first strand of the tassel across each of the remaining three gaps.

## Extra Info.....

You will be adding new lengths of thread to the work quite often in a design like this, but it is important you do not block the holes in the beads with knots. Use a keeper bead on the end of the new thread but do not knot onto the threads between the beads - just draw the new thread through five or six beads to where you need to restart and continue. When the work is complete go back to knot these ends into the work securely.

# 16

The needle will be emerging from through the first D bead threaded through in step 13. You can now work the needle around the tassel supports just made to add the second strands to the tassels.

Pass the needle down through the 1A, 1B, 1A, 3C, 1A, 1B, 1A and 1F beads of the first tassel support to emerge immediately above the first tassel strand made (fig 18).

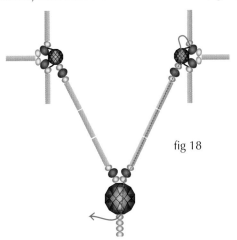

fig 18

Thread on 20A, 2C, 1A, 1B, 1A, 1E, 1A, 1B and 4A. Leaving aside the last 3A beads to anchor the strand pass the needle back up through the first 1A of the 4A just added and the following 1B, 1A, 1E, 1A, 1B, 1A, 2C, 20A and 1F. Pass the needle up through the 1A, 1B, 1A, 3C, 1A, 1B and 1A of the other side of the V-shaped tassel support. As in fig 17 pass the needle up through the D bead and across the beads of this grid arm to emerge pointing downwards from the corresponding D bead on the other edge of the arm.

Repeat step 16 three more times to add a 20A strand to each of the other three tassels.

Repeat step 16 four more times to add the third tassel strand from each support - this time use a count of 30A instead of 20A at the top of the tassel strand. Finish off the thread end.

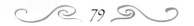

**17** The Central Tassel - Prepare the needle with 1.5m of single thread and tie a keeper bead 15cm from the end. Thread on 1B, 1G, 30A, 2C, 1A, 1B, 1A, 1E, 1A, 1B and 3A. Leaving aside the last 3A beads threaded to anchor the strand pass the needle back up through the 1B, 1A, 1E, 1A, 1B, 1A, 2C, 30A, 1G and 1B beads to emerge alongside the keeper bead (fig 19).

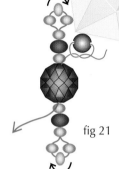

30A in total

fig 19

**18** Thread on 5A. Pick up the bauble and examine the bottom bead sequence where the four arms of the grid come together. Locate the C beads added in fig 12. Pass the needle through one of these C beads.

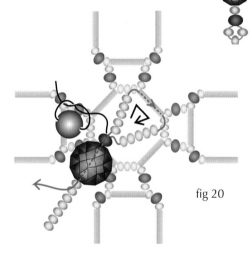

fig 20

Thread on 5A and pass the needle back through the 1B and 1G beads at the top of the tassel (fig 20).

**Note** - if you have made the sizing adjustment as suggested at the end of step 12 you will only pass through 1B bead on the base of the bauble instead of 1C.

**19** Examine the connection between the top of the tassel and the bauble grid. In step 20 you will need to make two more 5A straps to connect up to the opposite C bead on the bottom of the bauble which will centre the tassel at the bottom of the decoration. If, in fig 14, you used more than the stated 3A beads to tighten up the beading 5A beads may not be quite enough to stretch across the bottom of the bauble without putting a strain on the thread. If you need to adjust the bead count up to 6A or 7A unpick step 18 and remake with the new bead count.

**20** Thread on 40A, 2C, 1A, 1B, 1A, 1E, 1A, 1B and 4A. Leaving aside the last 3A beads threaded to anchor the strand pass the needle back up through the first 1A of the 4A just added and the following 1B, 1A, 1E, 1A, 1B, 1A, 2C, 40A, 1G and 1B to emerge alongside the keeper bead. Thread on 5A (or the new bead count as adjusted in step 19) and pass the needle through the 1C bead from fig 12 that sits opposite the C bead passed through in fig 20. Thread on 5A (or your new count) and pass the needle back down the 1B and 1G at the top of the tassel.

**21** Make the final tassel strand as before using a count of 50A instead of the 40A used previously. Bring the needle through to the top of the tassel to emerge alongside the keeper bead.

Remove the keeper bead and finish off both of the thread ends securely.

Finish off all the remaining thread ends.

**22** The Hanging Loop - Prepare the needle with 1.5m of single thread and tie a keeper bead 15cm from the end.

Thread on 1E, 1A, 1B and 4A. Leaving aside the last 3A threaded to anchor the strand pass the needle back through the first 1A of the 4A just added and the following 1B, 1A and 1E. Thread on 1A, 1B and 4A. As before, leave aside the last 3A beads to anchor the strand and pass the needle back through the preceeding 1A, 1B, 1A and 1E (fig 21).

Pass the needle through the following 1A, 1B and 4A (fig 22).

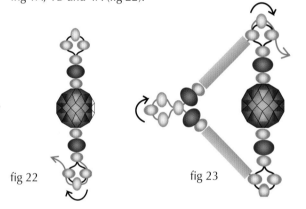

fig 21

fig 22                    fig 23

**23** Thread on 1C, 1A, 1B and 4A. Leaving aside the last 3A threaded to anchor the strand pass the needle back through the first 1A of the 4A just added (see fig 23). Thread on 1B, 1A and 1C. Pass the needle through the 3A beads of the anchor at the other end of the beading (fig 23).

## 24

Repeat step 23 to complete the diamond shape around the E bead. Finish with the needle emerging from the middle A bead of the anchor (fig 24).

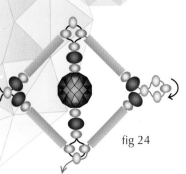

fig 24

fig 25

## 25

Thread on 1A, 1B, 1G, 1B and 1A.

Pass the needle through the loop at the top of the bauble and back up through the 1A, 1B, 1G and 1B beads just added.

Thread on 1A. Pass the needle, in the same direction as before, through the 1A bead at the bottom of the anchor that the needle emerged from at the beginning of this step (fig 25).

Pass the needle through all of the beads just added a second time to strengthen the connection. If the needle will pass through the holes again, repeat, to make the work as strong as possible.

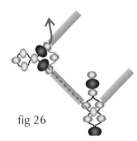

fig 26

## 26

Referring to fig 26 pass the needle up through the adjacent 1A and the following 1C and 1A beads. Thread on 1A and pass through the 1A bead immediately before the next C bead to pull the new A bead into the inner corner of the diamond shape (fig 26).

40A in total

fig 27

## 27

Pass the needle through the following 1C and 2A beads to emerge at the top of the diamond. Thread on 1A, 1B and 40A. Pass the needle back down the 1B bead to draw up the loop and thread on 1A. Pass the needle through the A bead at the top of the diamond in the same direction as before to centre the loop at the top of the diamond (see fig 27).

Pass the needle through the beads just added two more times to make sure that the strengthen the hanging loop.

Pass the needle through the following 1A, 1C and 1A down the other side of the diamond and thread on 1A. As on the first side of the diamond pass the needle through the 1A bead immediately before the next 1C to draw the new 1A into the inner corner of the diamond (fig 27). Pass the needle through the following 1C.

Finish off all the remaining thread ends securely.

# Byzantium Inspirations

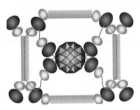

fig 28

The red bauble above does not have any tassel strands - instead the decoration is concentrated on the bauble itself. The cross-shaped grid has been worked and attached to the bauble as steps 1-12. The centre of each square on the grid is then enhanced with a cross-over stitch to add 1E bead (fig 28).

For a really bejewelled design add a short grid section between each of the arms to form a decorative band around the equator of the bauble.

# Sparkling Icicle

## You Will Need

### Materials

10g of size 10/0 silver lined crystal seed beads A
4g of size 3 silver lined crystal bugle beads B
Thirty-five 4mm crystal fire polished faceted beads C
Two 6mm crystal fire polished faceted beads D
One 12mm crystal fire polished faceted bead E
One 20mm crystal glass donut F
One sieve disc with nineteen holes
A reel of white size D beading thread

### Tools

A size 10 beading needle
A pair of scissors to trim the threads

The cascade of faceted beads throughout the icicle tassel glisten and glint in the light. This decoration is at its best when made in profusion and hung from the tree or bare branches collected from the garden. They are easy to make and a good introduction to decorative beading for the beginner as you will get a spectacular result with a minimum of practice.

The Decoration is Made in Three Stages

Firstly the sieve is decorated with sixteen tassel strands. The sieve is then pulled up to the donut so you can add the hanging loop.
Finally a second layer of fringe strands and spikes are added to cascade down over the edge of the donut.

1 The Sieve - Prepare the needle with 2m of single thread. Tie the end of the thread to the centre of the sieve so that you can bring the needle through to the outside curve of the sieve through the centre hole. Making the tassel uses quite a lot of thread - you will need to join on new lengths when necessary. It is easy to tie new threads onto the sieve just make sure that the cut ends of the thread are on the inner side of the cupped sieve so they will be concealed by the donut when the icicle is assembled.

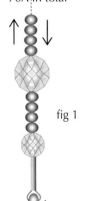

70A in total

fig 1

2 Thread on 70A, 1D, 4A, 1C, 1B and 1A. Leaving aside the last A bead threaded to anchor the strand pass the needle back up through the rest of the strand to emerge through the centre hole of the sieve (fig 1). Adjust the tension of the strand so that it falls softly but no thread shows between the beads or against the sieve.

3 Pass the needle down through one of the holes adjacent to the central hole of the sieve. Thread on 62A, 1C, 1B and 1A. Leaving aside the last A bead threaded to anchor the strand pass the needle back up through the rest of the beads and out through the same hole on the sieve.

4 There are five more holes around the central hole of the sieve. Each of these holes needs to have a tassel strand hanging from it. The tassel will look too regular if the strands are all the same length or if they are made in a pattern (one long; one short; one long etc) - the lengths need to be varied.

Pass the needle down the next hole around the centre and thread on a quantity of A between 44A and 62A followed by 1C, 1B and 1A. Leaving aside the last A bead threaded to anchor the strand pass the needle back up through the other beads as before to emerge through the same hole on the sieve. Thread down the third hole around the centre of the sieve.

Make a third tassel strand as the previous one using a different number of A beads (between 44A and 62A) to vary the length. Repeat for the last three holes around the centre of the sieve.

5 There are twelve further holes around the edge of the sieve. Each of these holes needs a further tassel strand. They are made to the same recipe as the previous six strands but with a quantity of A beads between 19A and 38A above the C bead.

You have an extra 3C beads available to you if you want to add a second tassel strand from any of the outer holes to 'fill out' the tassel shape. Make any extra tassel strand as before but take care not to pull the thread too tight which will distort the path of the existing tassel strand through the sieve hole. Finish off the thread securely.

fig 2

6 The Hanging Loop - Prepare the needle with 1.5m of thread. Bring the two cut ends together and tie a knot 2cm from the ends to double up the thread. Pass the needle down through one of the holes in the sieve around the central hole and back up through the central hole. Pass the needle through the loop of thread formed by the knot and pull up to tighten (fig 2).

**7** Pass the needle through the glass donut, 1E, 6A, 1D and 70A. Pass the needle back down the D bead to bring the 70A up into a loop (fig 3). Pass down through the following 6A, 1E, the donut and the central hole in the sieve and pull the thread to tension the whole ensemble so the sieve pulls up flat below the donut and the E bead fits snugly into the donut hole. Pass the needle up through one of the holes of the sieve around the central hole and up through the donut and the E bead again (this is a little fiddly as you must avoid snagging the tassel strands and find the hole in the facet).

Make a double knot with the needle thread to the threads between the beads at that point. Pass the needle up through a few A beads and repeat the knot. Pass through a few more beads before trimming to neaten the end of the thread.

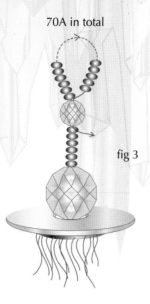

70A in total

fig 3

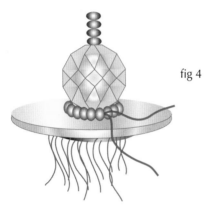

fig 4

**8** The Fringe & Spikes - Prepare the needle with 1.5m of single thread. Thread on 24 to 26A beads and drape around the junction between the E bead and the donut. This band of beads needs to fit closely into the crevice with no thread showing, but not so loose that the bead ring can slip up over the E bead. Adjust the bead count up or down until you are happy and tie the beads into a secure ring around the junction of the E bead and the donut (fig 4).

**9** Thread on 21A, 1C, 1B and 1A. Leaving aside the last A bead to anchor the strand pass the needle back up the 1B, 1C and 10A only. Thread on 11A and pass the needle through the second A bead around the ring of beads (fig 5). This is the first fringe strand.

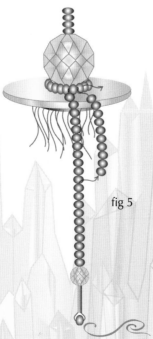

fig 5

**10** You will need to fringe around the rest of the ring of beads, but again you will need to vary the length of the strands.. As you proceed you will cover up the edge of the donut as the strands drape down into place.

**11** For the next strand thread on between 12A and 20A beads, 1C, 1B and 1A. Leaving aside the last A to anchor the strand pass the needle back up the B and C beads and a 'number' of A beads. This number will vary with your chosen length of fringe strand - if you have chosen 15A the number that you thread back up may be 5A, 7A or 8A for example - the choice is yours. You must, however, follow this number up with the correct amount of new A beads to make up the return strand length to that of the strand going down to the faceted bead ie. 15A down; thread back up through 8A; add 7 new A beads (8+7 = 15) (fig 6).

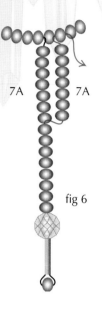

7A      7A

fig 6

Having added the remaining A beads to get back up to the ring pass the needle through the second A bead around the ring. Repeat all around the ring to make between ten and fifteen fringe strands (this will depend on the number of A beads in the ring).

**12** To make the spikes you will need to work back into the ring of beads around the E bead. Push all of the fringe strands out of the way over the edge of the donut. Thread on 1A, 1B and 1A. Leave aside the last A to anchor the end of the spike and pass back down the B bead and the following A bead. Pass the needle through the second A bead around the ring and pull the thread quite taught to make the first spike (fig 7).

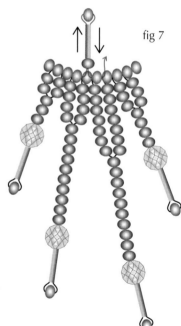

fig 7

**13** The lengths of the spikes need to vary a little although there is less licence in the number of beads that look effective. For the next spike thread on between 1A and 4A followed by 1B and 1A. Leave aside the last A bead and pass back down the B bead and the following A bead(s) to make the second spike - pull into place by passing the needle through the second A bead around the ring.

Repeat around the ring until you have between ten and fifteen spikes. Finish off the thread ends securely.

# Christmas Earrings

Christmas
Tree
Earrings

Santa
Earrings

four designs for
festive earrings

Angel
Earrings

Christmas
Pudding
Earrings

# Christmas Pudding Earrings

A calorie-free version of everyone's favourite course on the Christmas menu, but it does mean no brandy sauce until the big day! This method of covering a larger bead with smaller beads is quick and easy - a good method to consider for further investigation on other projects.

## You Will Need

### Materials

2g of DB 769 matt transparent brown Delica beads
0.4g of DB010 shiny black Delica beads
1g of DB201 ceylon white Delica beads B
0.4g of DB148 silver lined green Delica beads C
2g of size 8/0 silver lined red seed beads D
1g of size 8/0 black seed beads E
Two 12mm dark brown or black wooden beads
Two 50mm headpins
A pair of earfittings
A reel of black size D beading thread
A scrap of paper approx 4cm x 2cm

### Tools

A size 10 beading needle
A pair of scissors to trim the threads

## Each Earring is Made in Three Stages

First you will cover the wooden bead with the brown and black Delicas.
The covered bead is then pinned and looped.
The brandy sauce, holly leaves and berries are added as the final flourish.

**1** Covering the Wooden Bead - Mix the brown and the black Delicas together to give a plum pudding selection to work from - call this mixture A. These A beads are wrapped over the larger wooden bead with the needle passing through the hole in the wooden bead. When you are covering a larger bead in this way the small beads always tend to run into the hole of the larger bead sabotaging the process so you will need to make a plug for the larger bead.

Take a small piece of paper approximately 4cm x 2cm and tightly roll to make a tube 4cm long. Push this into the hole in the wooden bead (fig 1). This tube will allow the needle to pass down between the wall of the hole and the paper but prevent any of the smaller beads from following.

fig 1

Prepare the needle with 1.5m of single thread and tie a keeper bead 15cm from the end.

**2** Pass the needle up through the hole in the wooden bead and thread on 14A. Pass the needle up through the hole in the wooden bead again to bring the strap of A beads around the wooden bead (fig 2). Repeat once more so that you have two straps.

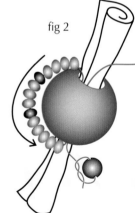

fig 2

**3** Bring the needle through the first 3A beads of the second strap and thread on 8A. Pass the needle through the last 3A beads on the same strap and up through the wooden bead (fig 3). This short strap will help to fill out the circumference of the wooden bead. Repeat all around the wooden bead making two straps of 14A first and then adding a short strap of 8A to the second of the two straps just completed.

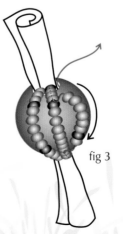

fig 3

You will need approximately five repeats until the wooden bead is reasonably covered with A beads. If necessary go back and add a few short 8A straps to fill any gaps. Leave the thread attached.

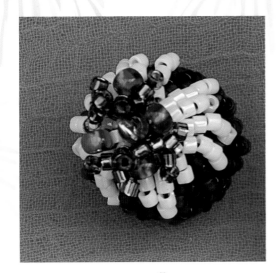

**7** The Holly Leaves and Berries - Bring the needle out as close as possible to the D bead below the loop. Thread on 3C. Pass the needle up through the second C bead just threaded to bring the third C bead up as an anchor (fig 6).

fig 6                                    fig 7

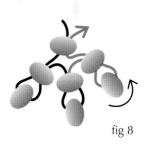

**8** Thread on 2C and thread back up the first of the 2C just added to make a second branch (fig 7). Thread on 2C and pass up the first C of the 2C just added and the very first C bead of the sequence (fig 8) to complete the leaf. Pass the needle through an adjacent B bead close to the D bead.

fig 8

Repeat three or four times around the top of the pudding.

Add single D beads into the gaps between the leaves to form the berries.

**9** Finish off the thread securely and neaten before trimming. Attach the needle to the other end of the thread and finish off similarly.

Repeat to make a second pudding.

Add the earfittings to complete the earrings.

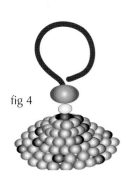

fig 4

**4** Adding the Headpin - Thread 1E onto a headpin. Carefully remove the paper tube and insert the headpin so that the E bead pulls up close to the bottom hole of the wooden bead. Thread onto the top of the pin 1E, 1B and 1D. Push these beads down so that the E bead nestles down onto the hole at the top of the wooden bead and so that no A beads can fall into the hole.

Trim the headpin to 8mm above the D bead and make a loop (fig 4).

If you are not sure how to make a loop see page 16.

**5** Bring the needle through the A beads if necessary to emerge alongside the keeper bead. Remove the keeper bead and tie this end of the thread to the needle end pulling the knot up closely to the beadwork to conceal - do not trim the thread ends yet. Reposition the needle to emerge from the A beads at the top of the pudding.

**6** Adding the Brandy Sauce - The sauce is made up from a series of random length stitches attached to the A beads of the first layer. Thread on 5B; count down 5A on the nearest strand of A beads and pass the needle through these 5A to emerge at the top of the A bead strap (fig 5). Thread on 4B and repeat to attach to the first 4A of the next strap around to make the next 'drizzle' of sauce.

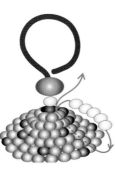

fig 5

Repeat around the top of the pudding adding sauce strands of between 2 and 5B to most of the A bead straps - do not add to all of the straps as the beading will become too bunched. If necessary add a few single B beads to fill in any gaps around the top to conceal the E bead. Leave the thread end attached.

## Attaching A Fishhook Earwire

You must open the loop on the earwire to link it onto the top of the prepared earring dangle. Place your round nosed or snipe nosed pliers on the front of the loop at 90° to the spring above the bead. With your other hand grip as close as you can to the loop (placing your fingers over the bead and the spring). Roll (not pull) your plier wrist over just a little to gently twist the loop open. Attach the earring dangle and place the pliers back in the same position to roll the loop shut. Do not roll the loop open too far as the wire is quite stiff and can become brittle if you bend it too far.

# Angel Earrings

These pretty little angels are so lightweight you will not know you have them on your ears, so watch out, because everyone will want to steal them away. They are a year-round winner if you sing in a choir or they will stitch onto the top of a lapel pin for a more discreet display on your choristers' robes.

## You Will Need

### Materials

2.5g of DB201 ceylon white Delica beads A
2.5g of DB041 silver lined Delica beads B
0.2g of DB210 opaque pink or DB769 dark brown C
Two 6mm round glass beads to match C for the heads D
Two 7mm gold plated jump rings for the halos
Two 4mm silver plated jump rings
A pair of silver plated earfittings
A reel of white size D beading thread

### Tools

A size 13 beading needle
A pair of scissors to trim the threads
A pair of fine pliers to add the earfittings

Each Earring is Made in Seven Easy Stages
The body is made first.
The body supports the top of the skirt.
The wings attach to the back of the body.
The halo attaches to the back of the neck.
The arms link to either side of the body.
The head threads into place in front of the halo.
Finally the earfitting is added to the top of the head.

**2** Bring the first column around to sit alongside the fifth column. Pass the needle up through the first column, down the fifth and up the first column again to bring the five columns into a ring (fig 3). This completes the body of the angel.

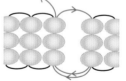

fig 3

**1** The Body - Prepare the needle with 1.5m of single thread and tie a keeper bead 15cm from the end. Thread on 6A. Pass the needle back down the first 3A beads to bring the second 3A parallel to the first 3A (fig 1). Pass the needle back up through the second 3A beads (fig 2). Thread on 3A. Pass the needle up through the second 3A and back down the 3A just added to bring the new 3A beads parallel to the second 3A - this is ladder stitch. Thread on 3A to make a fourth column. Repeat a fifth time to give five columns of 3A beads each.

**3** The Skirt - The bottom row of the body supports the skirt. Pass the needle down through one column of the body to bring the thread to the bottom edge. This bottom row needs to be increased to give a full skirt for the angel. Thread on 2A. Turn the needle and pass it back up through the bottom bead of the column that the needle emerged from (fig 4). Pull on the thread to bring the two new beads to sit parallel to one another at the bottom of the column. Pass the needle down through the bottom A bead of the next column along (fig 5) and repeat to add 2A beads to the bottom of this column. Repeat three more times to add 10A beads in total to the bottom row of the angel's body.

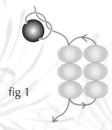

fig 1

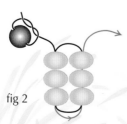

fig 2

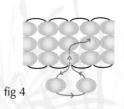

fig 4

fig 5

**4** Pass the needle down through the bottom bead of the next column along and out through one of the added A beads to begin the skirt strands. Thread 10A, 1B and 1A.

Leaving aside the last A bead threaded to anchor the strand turn the needle and pass it back up through the B bead. Pass the needle back up through the following 10A beads (fig 6).

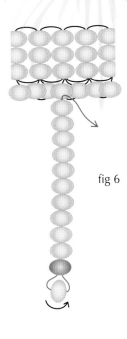

fig 6

Pass the needle up through the same A bead attached to the bottom of the column in step 3. Pass the needle down through the other A bead attached to the same column.

Repeat the strand bringing the needle out through the A bead at the top which was added in step 3.

Pass the needle down through one of the A beads attached to the bottom of the next column along.

Repeat the strand.

Repeat step 4 all around the base of the body to make ten skirt strands in total.

Bring the needle up through the three beads of one of the columns to emerge at the top edge.

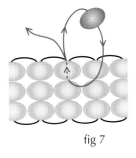

fig 7

fig 8

**5** The Wings - Thread on 1B and pass the needle back up through the top A bead of the same column (fig 7). Pass the needle back down the new B bead and thread on 1B. Pass the needle back up through the second A bead of this column (fig 8). Pass the needle back down the new B bead and thread on 1B - this is square stitch.

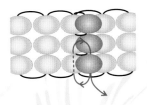

fig 9

Repeat as for the previous stitch to attach this B bead to the bottom A bead of this column - finish the stitch by passing the needle back down the new B bead (fig 9). This row of 3B is the foundation row for the wings.

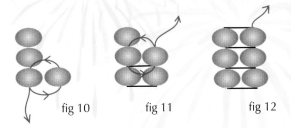

fig 10          fig 11          fig 12

**6** The next row of the wings is made in a similar way to the foundation row. Thread on 1B. Pass the needle down through the bottom B bead of the foundation row (fig 10). Pass the needle up through the new B bead and thread on 1B. Pass down the second B bead of the foundation row and back up the new B bead (fig 11). Repeat for a third B bead (fig 12). Reposition the needle by passing it right through the 3B of the first row and up the first B bead only of the new row (fig 13).

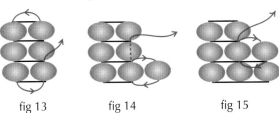

fig 13          fig 14          fig 15

**7** Thread on 1B. Pass the needle back up through the bottom B bead and the middle B bead of the previous row (fig 14). Thread on 1B and pass the needle up through the middle B bead of the previous row (fig 15). Pass the needle down through the new B bead and the B bead below it (fig 16).

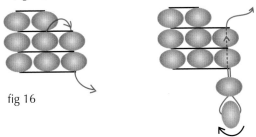

fig 16

fig 17

**8** Thread on 2B. Leaving aside the last bead threaded pass the needle back up through the first 1B just added and the 2B above (fig 17). Thread on 4B, and pass the needle back down the first 3B beads just added and the 2B beads attached to the previous row (fig 18). This makes the first set of wing ribs.

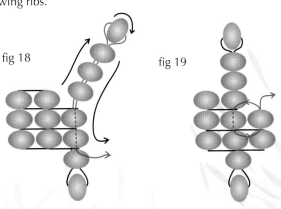

fig 18          fig 19

**9** Using the same technique as in step 8 square stitch two new B beads to the 2B beads of the previous row (fig 19).

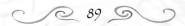

# 10

The needle will emerge through the top of the last B bead added. Thread on 6B and pass the needle back down the first 5B beads just added and the 2B attached to the previous row (fig 20). Thread on 4B and pass the needle back up the first 3B just added and out through the top of the 2B attached to the previous row (fig 21).

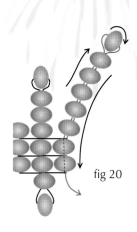

fig 20

Add two further B beads to the B beads of the previous row as before (fig 22).

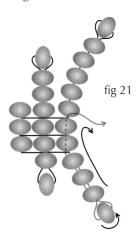

fig 21

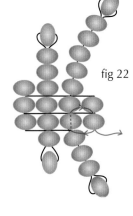

fig 22

# 11

The needle will be emerging to point downwards from the 2B beads just added. Thread on 5B and pass the needle up through the first 4B just added and the following 2B beads (fig 23).

fig 23

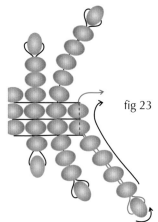

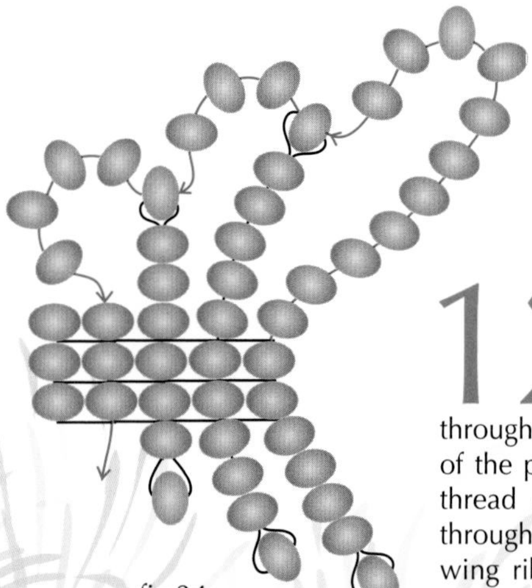

fig 24

# 12

Thread on 11B. Pass the needle through the top B bead of the previous wing rib; thread on 3B and pass through the top of the first wing rib. Thread on 4B and pass down through the first 3B of the wing (not the foundation row) (fig 24).

# 13

Pass the needle up through the 3B beads of the foundation row ready to begin the other wing.

You need to follow the instructions from step 6 but the needle is pointing in the opposite direction to that of the first wing so you will find that your needle direction is reversed. It does not make too much of a difference to the procedure, but, you will notice that you will have to make the top half of the first rib before the shorter bottom part and the opposite on the second rib. When you get to the last rib you will have change the procedure slightly.

The needle is pointing in the wrong direction so you will have to make the long portion of the rib first. Thread on 8B and pass the needle back through the first 7B threaded and the 2B that are attached to the previous row (fig 25).

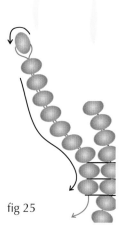

Thread on 5B to make the bottom half of the rib as before. Pass right back up to the top of the long rib and thread on 3B.

fig 25

Pass the needle through the top bead of the second rib. Complete this wing as for the first wing.

# 14

The Halo
Pass the needle back up the 3B beads of the wing foundation row and thread on 2B.

Pass through the centre of a 7mm jump ring and back down through the 2B beads just added (fig 26).

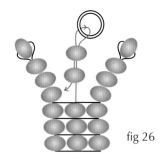

fig 26

Pass the needle on down through the 3B beads of the foundation row and up through the first 5B beads of an adjacent wing row.

# 15

Pass the needle down through the B bead below the halo and back up through the fifth B bead just emerged from (fig 27).

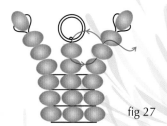

fig 27

Pass the needle down through the B bead below the halo again and attach it to the fifth B bead on the first rib of the other wing in a similar manner.

# 16

The Arms - Bring the needle down through the 2B beads below the halo and pass the needle into the top A bead of the column that the foundation row of the wings is attached to.

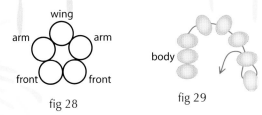

fig 28

fig 29

Pass the needle up through the top A bead of an adjacent column (see fig 28 - the top view of the body to check you have the needle in the correct place for the first arm). Thread on 5A and pass the needle back up through the fourth A bead just added to make the elbow (fig 29).

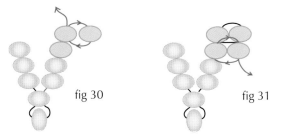

fig 30

fig 31

# 17

Thread on 2A and 2C. Thread on a further 1C and pass the needle back through the second C bead in the same direction as before (fig 30). Pass back down the new C bead a second time. Thread on 1C and pass the needle back up the first C bead threaded to bring the new C bead alongside the first C bead. Pass the needle back down the fourth C bead (fig 31).

# 18

Thread on 4A and pass the needle up through the third A bead just added to make the second elbow. Thread on 3A (fig 32). Arrange the arms so that the elbows point downwards towards the skirt.

fig 32

Pass the needle down the top A bead of the body on the other side of the wings. Work the needle down to emerge through the bottom A bead of that column. Pass the needle up through the A bead of the arm just above the elbow and back down the A bead on the column to hold the arm in place.

Work the needle across to the other side of the body and attach the other arm similarly.

# 19

The Head - Pass the needle through the beads of an adjacent column so that it emerges beneath the skirt underneath the body. Thread on 1A and pass the needle up through the hole in the middle of the body tube (fig 33).

fig 33

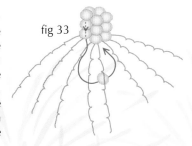

# 20

Thread on 1A, 1D and 1A. Pass the needle through a small jump ring and back down the top A bead (fig 34), the D bead and the A bead below it. Pass through the hole in the centre of the body.

Secure the thread by passing through one of the beads at the very top of the skirt and thread back up through the body, the A bead below the D bead and the D bead itself to emerge immediately below the top A bead.

fig 34

# 21

Bring the halo up behind the D bead. Pass the needle through the halo and back down the head D bead and the neck A bead below it (fig 35).

Pass the needle down through a few beads of the body and secure with a double knot.

Neaten the thread end and trim.

fig 35

Return to the keeper bead and remove it. Attach the needle to this end of the thread and finish off this thread end in a similar manner to the other end of thread. Pass the needle through a few beads before trimming.

# 22

Attaching the Earwire - Twist open the loop on the earfitting and attach to the top jump ring above the halo. Repeat for the second earring.

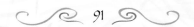

# Santa Earrings

We guarantee a smile across the face of everyone you meet when you are wearing these earrings but don't just confine them to your earlobes - make one without the top loop and it glue onto a tietack for Dad to wear on Christmas Day. To make the Santa earrings you will need to be able to work in brick stitch and follow a simple grid. If you have not worked with brick stitch before please refer to the brick stitch instructions on page 9.

## Each Earring is Made in Four Stages
The flat brick stitch grid is worked first with the additional extension for the hat and the loop for the earfitting.
The three dimensional beard, moustache and nose are applied next.
The pom-pom at the end of the hat is added.
Finally the earfitting is hooked onto the top.

**1** The pattern grid in fig 1 shows the brick stitch pattern for the first layer of beading. The numbers on some of the white beads show the position and length of the A bead fringe strands that fill out the beard and moustache. The separate block to the side of the main grid is the extension to the hat.

Prepare your needle with 3m of single thread and tie a keeper bead 1m from the end. The long end of the thread will be used first to make the lower part of the pattern and the beard strands - you will then return to the 1m portion of the thread to work the top half of the grid including the hat and pom-pom.

## You Will Need

### Materials

2.5g of DB201 ceylon white Delica beads A
1g of DB602 silver lined red Delica beads B
1g of DB210 pink opaque Delica beads C
0.1g of DB047 silver lined blue Delica beads D
Two 4mm white or clear round glass beads E
Two 4mm jump rings
A pair of earfittings
A reel of white size D beading thread

### Tools

A size 13 beading needle
A pair of scissors to trim the threads
A pair of fine pliers to add the earfittings

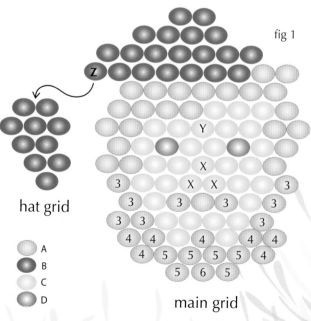

fig 1

hat grid

- A
- B
- C
- D

main grid

**2** The Grid - The row marked Z on the grid (fig 1) is the foundation row and should be worked in ladder stitch. Work down through the pattern to the bottom of the chin in brick stitch. Bring the needle down through the centre bead at the base of the chin to finish.

**3** The Beard - Thread on 6A as indicated on the grid for this bead. Leaving aside the last A bead threaded to anchor the strand; pass the needle back up through the remaining 5A just added to make the central fringe strand. Pass the needle back up through the A bead at the bottom of the chin (fig 2).

Do not pull the thread too tightly - the fringe strand needs to hang softly.

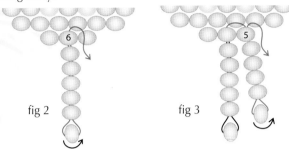

fig 2                fig 3

**4** Pass the needle down through the adjacent A bead on the base of the chin (marked with a 5 on the grid). Thread on the 5A as indicated and repeat as with the 6A to make the second fringe strand (fig 3) bringing the needle out through the top of the chin bead to complete the stitch.

**5** The fringe strands now need to be repeated across all the indicated beard beads of the grid. Move the needle through the beading to reach each of the indicated beads in turn - it is important that the needle always begins the strand pointing downwards out of the indicated grid bead or the strands will not lie correctly.

Leave the three moustache beads (underneath the three X beads of the nose) until stage 6.

**6** The Moustache - Bring the needle downwards through one of the end beads of the moustache and make the 3A bead strand as indicated on the main grid. Bring the needle back up through the original moustache bead marked 3 on the grid to complete the strand.
Thread on 1A and pass the needle upwards through the single grid bead a second time to bring the new bead to sit on top of the original one (fig 4).

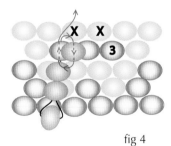

fig 4

Repeat at the other end of the moustache.

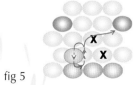

fig 5

fig 6

**7** The Nose - Bring the needle upwards through one of the beads marked X on the grid. Thread on 1C. Pass the needle up through the X bead a second time to bring the new bead to sit on top of the original one (fig 5). Repeat to add a single C bead on top of the other two X beads on the grid.

**8** Reposition the needle to emerge through one of the two lower nose beads just applied. Pass the needle in a square stitch through the two lower nose beads (fig 6) to link these two beads together. Pass the needle up through the other new C bead (fig 7).

Thread on 1C and pass the needle up through the bead marked Y on the grid to taper the 3D nose between the eyes.

fig 7

**9** Pass the needle through the beads of the grid to emerge towards the lower half of the design. Make a double knot here to secure the thread and neaten the thread end by passing through a few beads before trimming.

**10** The Hat - Untie the keeper bead left at Z and reattach the needle. Work the remaining three rows of the main grid up to the top of the hat. Bring the needle out through the top of one of the two red beads on the top of the hat.

Thread on 4B and pass the needle down through the adjacent B bead on the top of the hat to make a loop for the earfitting (fig 8).

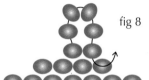

fig 8

**11** Work the needle through the beads of the grid to emerge pointing downwards from the bead marked Z on the grid. You now need to work the extra little grid of B beads - follow the hat extension grid downwards to add 2B for the first row. The second row adds 3B etc. As you work you will see that this small grid of beads overlaps the edge of the larger main grid to emphasise the 3D effect. Bring the needle out through the bottom of the lowest bead of the hat grid to begin the pom-pom.

**12** Thread on 1E and 4A. Push the beads up closely to the bottom of the hat. Pass the needle through the E bead a second time to bring the A beads into a strap around the E bead (fig 9).

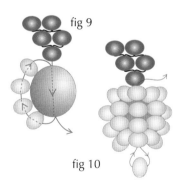

fig 9

fig 10

**13** Thread on 4A and pass the needle down through the E bead again to make a second strap. Repeat five more times to cover the E bead with seven straps of A beads. With the needle emerging from the bottom of the pom-pom thread on 1A. Turn the needle and pass it back up through the E bead to bring the single A bead into a stopper at the base of the E bead and conceal the hole (fig 10). Pass the needle back up into the red beads of the hat and finish off the thread end securely.

**14** Attaching the Earwires - Twist open the first jump ring and attach the first earfitting to the loop made in step 10. Repeat to make the second earring - flip the face over before you start the beard fringes so that you make a mirror image of the first earring.

# Christmas Tree Earrings

These little three-dimensional trees are a delight to wear – make them in silver and crystal beads instead of green, red and gold for an incredibly glamorous look to go with your Christmas party dress. To make the tree earrings you will need to be able to work in brick stitch and follow a simple grid. If you have not worked with brick stitch before please refer to the brick stitch instructions on page 9.

## You Will Need

### Materials

2.5g of DB605 silver lined green Delica beads A
0.5g of silver lined red size 15/0 seed beads B
0.2g of silver lined gold size 15/0 seed beads C
Two 7mm metallic star beads D
Two 6mm fire polished faceted beads E
Two 4mm gold plated jump rings
A pair of gold plated earfittings
A reel of emerald size D beading thread

### Tools

A size 13 beading needle
A pair of scissors to trim the threads
A pair of fine pliers to add the earfittings
A small amount of clear-drying nail polish
to stiffen the beadwork when complete

## Each Earring is Made in Five Stages

The trunk beads are threaded and the first axis of the tree is worked in brick stitch.
The second axis of the tree is added followed by the third.
The pot is added to the bottom of the design and the star to the top.
The trimmings complete the beading.
The branches are stiffened to make the design more robust.

**1** Prepare the needle with 2m of single thread and tie a keeper bead 15cm from the end. Thread on 17A to form the trunk.

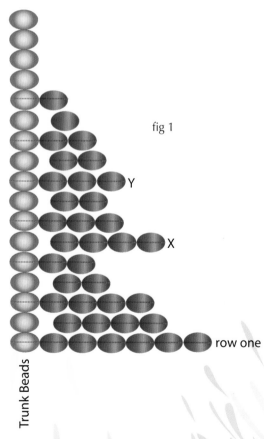

fig 1

Y

X

Trunk Beads

row one

**2** The Trunk and First Axis -The chart in fig 1 shows the bead sequence for one axis of the tree together with the straight row of beads for the trunk.

Work horizontally from the last bead of the trunk to make a ladder stitched foundation row 6A long (fig 2) as shown on the chart.

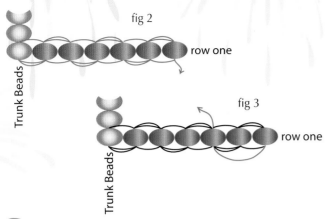

fig 2

Trunk Beads

row one

fig 3

Trunk Beads

row one

**3** To begin the second row bring the needle up through the third A bead from the end of the foundation row (fig 3) and start with a two bead stitch. Work the other two beads of the row as shown on the chart.

**4** Begin the third row with a two bead stitch. You will see from the chart that this row is linked onto the trunk - pass the needle back down the new bead nearest the trunk and up through the third bead from the bottom of the trunk. Pass the needle down the bead adjacent to the trunk and up through the second of the two new beads (fig 4). Every second row will need to be linked to the corresponding trunk bead in a similar manner. Work the two beads to the end of the row.

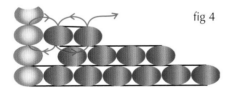

fig 4

Reposition the needle for the next row and work the two beads as indicated.

Follow the pattern up to and including the top row joining the alternate rows onto the trunk as you proceed.

**5** The Second and Third Axis - Pass the needle down through the beads of the trunk to emerge through the bottom bead. Begin the second axis with a horizontal ladder stitched foundation row of 6A as in step 2. Work to the top of this axis.

Bring the needle down through the beads of the trunk to start the final axis of the tree. Work this axis as for the previous two axes bringing the needle right down through the beads of the trunk when the third axis is complete. Position the axes at 120° to one another.

**6** The Pot and the Star - Thread on 1A, 1E and 1A. Turn the needle and pass it back up through the E bead pulling the last A bead threaded into an anchor for the strand. Pass the needle up through the next A bead and all the A beads of the trunk to emerge at the top of the trunk.

**7** Thread on 1D and 1A. Pass the needle through one of the jump rings and back down the last A bead threaded and the following D bead to emerge alongside the keeper bead.

Remove the keeper bead and tie the two ends of the thread together securely drawing the knots down between the beads at that point to conceal.

Pass the needle through a few beads of the trunk to neaten before trimming. Attach the needle onto the other end of the thread and neaten and trim similarly.

**8** The Trimmings - Prepare the needle with 1m of single thread and tie a keeper bead 15cm from the end. Pass the needle up through the bead marked X on the end of one of the branches of the three axes. * Thread on 1C. Turn the needle and pass it back down through the X bead on the end of the branch (fig 5). Thread on 12B. Pass the needle up through the X bead on the next axis around. Repeat from * twice more to complete three swags of B beads between the axes and three C bead baubles sitting on top of the X beads. Pass the needle through the C bead on the top of the first X bead and down through the X bead. Remove the keeper bead and tie this end of the thread to the other as before. Neaten the thread ends by passing through a few beads before trimming.

fig 5

**9** Repeat to make 9B bead swags around the Y beads of the three axes adding a C bead bauble to the top of each Y bead as you go.

Attach an earwire to the jump ring at the top of the tree and repeat to make a second earring.

**10** Stiffening the Tree Branches - Hang the earrings up from the earhooks and straighten out the three axes on each tree to be at 120° to one another. Carefully paint the A beads of the axes and the trunks with a thin coat of clear nail polish. Try not to get the polish onto the B bead swags. Leave to dry and repeat with a second coat. The thin coats of polish will trickle between the beads and onto the threads which will stiffen as the polish dries. Two coats should be sufficient but you can add a further coat if you wish.

# Index & Suppliers

All of the materials used in this book should be available in any good bead shop or online. If you are new to beading, or need more supplies, the companies listed below run fast, efficient mail order services, hold large stocks of all of the materials you will need in their stores and give good, well-informed friendly advice on aspects of beading and beading needs.

### In the UK

**Spellbound Bead Co**
47 Tamworth Street,
Lichfield
Staffordshire
WS13 6JW
01543 417650

www.spellboundbead.co.uk

Spellbound Bead Co supplied all of the materials for the samples shown. You can buy the beads loose (wholesale and retail) for all of the designs or in kit form (with or without instructions) for most of the designs.

### In USA

**Fire Mountain Gems**
One Fire Mountain Way
Grants Pass
OR 97526 - 2373
Tel: + 800 355 2137
www.firemountaingems.com

**Shipwreck Beads**
8560 Commerce Place Dr.NE
Lacey
WA 98516
Tel: + 800 950 4232
www.shipwreckbeads.com

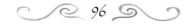